BUILT ON
FAITH

A Young Christian's Guide to Unshakable Character

TYSON GENTRY

Foreword by Joel Penton

To Adam and Ryan,

You are my greatest blessings. My prayer is that your faith will be your foundation and your character, your compass. I hope to help guide you through the ups and downs of life, but even if I'm not beside you, trust that my love is with you every step of the way.

24 Productions
12850 Highway 9
Suite 600–238
Alpharetta, GA 30004

Paperback ISBN: 979-8-9889453-7-6
Hardcover ISBN: 979-8-9889453-8-3
eBook ISBN: 979-8-9889453-9-0

THE HOLY BIBLE, NEW INTERNATIONAL VERSION®, NIV© Copyright © 1973, 1978, 1984, 2011 by Biblica, Inc.® Used by permission. All rights reserved worldwide.

Interior layout design by Pix Bee Design (pixbeedesign.com)

This book is available in quantity at special discount for your school, group, or church. For further information, please contact via: tysongentry.com.

Printed in the U.S.A.

24

24 Productions

TABLE OF CONTENTS

Foreword

By Joel Penton

In a world where the character of young people is constantly being tested, Built on Faith arrives as both a timely guide and a lasting resource. This book speaks directly to students, offering not just biblical knowledge, but a practical path toward spiritual and personal growth.

Built on Faith is written by a special person. I've had the privilege of knowing Tyson Gentry for more than 20 years. He is a man of the highest character—someone who not only teaches these values but lives them daily. His integrity, humility, and quiet strength have had a profound impact on my own life, and I have no doubt this book will impact yours.

In his book Tyson reinforces foundational traits that we at LifeWise Academy teach our students every day—trust, courage, integrity, humility, and many others. These lessons are more than theoretical. Tyson shares real-life examples and offers concrete challenges that bring faith into action.

This book isn't just for students. It's a valuable tool for parents and educators who are walking alongside young believers, helping them navigate the formative years with wisdom and purpose. With its thoughtful reflection questions and action steps, Built on Faith invites personal introspection, calling everyone to go deeper in their relationship with Christ and apply biblical principles in everyday situations.

Whether used in the classroom, at home, or in personal study, this book will help shape young hearts for years to come. I'm grateful for the impact Tyson continues to have, and I believe you will be, too.

Joel Penton

Introduction

If you're holding this book, it means you're ready to build something important—something that shapes every area of your life. This isn't a book about quick fixes or temporary changes. It's about building a foundation of strong, lasting character that's firmly rooted in faith.

Why is character so important? Because character doesn't just shape who you are—it *is* who you are. It impacts your faith, your relationship with God, your friendships, and your family life. It guides your choices, opens new opportunities, and plays a key role in your ability to achieve fulfillment and success. Your character is deeply influenced by what you believe and how you put those beliefs into practice each day.

The chapters ahead explore essential qualities that form the core of your character—qualities like resilience, integrity, patience, humility, generosity, and much more. Each chapter will guide you through practical examples, thoughtful reflections, and actionable steps to help you apply and internalize these important traits.

A Note About the Journey Ahead

This book is more than a collection of character traits—it's a journey of growth. Each chapter builds upon the one before it, guiding you through a natural and meaningful progression. It begins with the foundation of faith, then moves into trust and obedience, which are essential for any relationship with God. From there, you'll develop inner strength through conviction, courage, self-discipline, and integrity, before facing life's challenges with resilience, perseverance, and patience.

As you grow, you'll learn the power of humility, gratitude, and finally, grace—a turning point that shifts the focus outward. The second half of this journey emphasizes how we treat others, with chapters on respect and generosity, leading into confidence, accountability, and finally, leadership. By the end, you won't just understand these character traits—you'll be equipped to live them out in a way that honors God, strengthens your relationships, and impacts the world around you.

While each chapter focuses on a specific trait, you'll quickly notice how interconnected they all are. Don't be surprised if some chapters overlap or echo ideas from others. That's intentional. True character isn't built in isolated pieces; it's woven together into a unified whole. Just like a strong tree requires healthy roots and sturdy branches, your character needs each of these qualities working together to truly flourish.

Take your time with each chapter. Engage thoughtfully with the questions at the end, reflect on the stories provided, and allow yourself to genuinely consider the concepts presented. Talk about what you're learning with family and friends, and apply these ideas to your everyday experiences. Some concepts may come naturally, while others may require patience and practice—that's part of the process, regardless of your age or stage in life.

If you want to get the most out of this book, don't skip over the Discussion Questions and Action Challenges at the end of each chapter. They're designed to help you dig deeper, connect the lessons to your own life, and take meaningful steps toward growth. The more you invest in these moments of reflection and practice, the more lasting your character development will be.

The tenets presented here aren't just suggestions—they're fundamental building blocks for a fulfilling, faith-filled life. They're keys to honoring God genuinely, treating people with love and respect, and handling life's ups and downs wisely.

As you start this journey, remember you're not alone. God is guiding your steps and helping you grow into the person He designed you to be. So, dive in with courage, openness, and anticipation. A life built on faith and strong character is waiting—and it's a journey worth taking, no matter where you are right now.

The chapters you're about to read mark the start of something much bigger—a lifelong process of building the kind of character that lasts.

CHAPTER 1

Faith

"Now faith is confidence in what we hope for and assurance about what we do not see."

– Hebrews 11:1 (New International Version)

Think about building a house. Before you even worry about buying wood or other materials, the very first thing you need to do is make sure you have a strong foundation. You can build the biggest and strongest house imaginable, but what that house is standing on is much more important than the house itself.

If the foundation is weak, it won't take much to compromise your structure and the whole house can easily collapse. But a strong foundation can withstand storms, fires, and earthquakes. Life is full of ups and downs, but if your life is built on faith in God, you can withstand anything.

"The rain came down...yet it did not fall, because it had its foundation on the rock." – Matthew 7:25

Faith should be the foundation of your character. Through-out your life, each of the character qualities discussed in this book will be challenged and tested. There will be times when your integrity, patience, humility, and even your generosity will face difficult moments and hard decisions.

But when your belief in God is strong and unwavering, you'll find the strength and wisdom to uphold these virtues. Your faith is the anchor that secures every other part of your character, and it will keep you steadfast—regardless of what life brings your way.

Quick Takeaway: With God as your foundation, you'll never face life's challenges alone.

What is Faith?

Faith is trusting that God is in control...even when life is uncertain. It's believing He knows exactly what you need, even if it's not always what you want or expect. Faith is more than feelings. It's a choice you make—every day—to trust God and build your life on His promises.

Your faith doesn't just appear instantly; it grows steadily through prayer, experiences, and studying God's Word. Like any strong relationship, your walk with God takes time, patience, and effort—but the reward is well worth it.

> *"Ask and it will be given to you; seek and you will find; knock and the door will be opened to you."*
>
> – Matthew 7:7

Why Do We Need Faith and a Savior?

God created a perfect world, but sin entered when Adam and Eve disobeyed God by eating from the tree of the knowledge of good and evil. This act brought sin into the world, separating humanity from God, and the world hasn't been the same since.

"Therefore, just as sin entered the world through one man, and death through sin, and in this way death came to all people, because all sinned." – Romans 5:12

In the times written about in the Old Testament, people had to sacrifice animals to temporarily pay for their sins, because:

"Without the shedding of blood there is no forgiveness."

– Hebrews 9:22

These sacrifices couldn't fully remove sin, which is why Jesus came as the perfect and final sacrifice.

Hundreds of years before He was born, prophecies foretold Jesus' birth, death, and resurrection—confirming He truly was the Savior sent by God. Here are a few examples of specific prophecies Jesus fulfilled:

† Born of a virgin (Isaiah 7:14 → Matthew 1:22-23)

† Born in Bethlehem (Micah 5:2 → Luke 2:4-7)

† Betrayed for silver (Zechariah 11:12 → Matthew 26:14-16)

† Pierced for our sins (Isaiah 53:5 → John 19:34)

† Risen from the dead (Psalm 16:10 → Matthew 28:5-6)

This is just a very quick summary of everything, but the point is we need a Savior because we can't bridge the gap created by sin. No matter how good or kind we try to be, we always fall short of God's perfect standard. God, in His great love for us, provided a way to restore our relationship with Him through Jesus.

Without Jesus' sacrifice, we would remain separated from God because sin cannot exist in His holy presence. Through Jesus, we receive forgiveness, restoration, and the promise of eternal life—gifts we could never earn, but are freely given because of His grace and love for us.

When Jesus died, He paid for our sins completely. His resurrection proved He conquered sin and death.

> "From that time on Jesus began to explain to his disciples that he must go to Jerusalem and suffer many things at the hands of the elders, the chief priests and the teachers of the law, and that he must be killed and on the third day be raised to life." – Matthew 16:21

How Can We Be Saved?

Being saved isn't about working harder or being good enough—it's about *believing* in Jesus and what He did for us. The Bible tells us clearly:

> "The work of God is this: to believe in the one he has sent." – John 6:29

Salvation is a gift we accept through faith:

> "If you declare with your mouth, 'Jesus is Lord,' and believe in your heart that God raised him from the dead, you will be saved." – Romans 10:9

The Bible teaches that without accepting Jesus as the one who died for your sins and rose again, you remain separated from God—and that separation lasts forever. Hell is real and it's not a place of second chances or peace; it's eternal separation from the love, presence, and hope of God. But once you believe in Him, nothing can separate you from God's love (Romans 8:38-39).

Faith Is a Marathon, Not a Sprint

Faith isn't just for Sunday mornings or big spiritual moments. It's needed every day—even ordinary days that feel repetitive. Sometimes faith feels strong and exciting, while other times it's quiet and discreet.

You won't always feel "on fire" for God. That's okay! Your faith isn't based on emotions—it's based on truth. God promises to always be there for you:

> *"Never will I leave you; never will I forsake you."*
>
> – Hebrews 13:5

Just like athletes train daily, even when tired, your faith needs regular practice. Pray when you don't feel like it, read the Bible when it's hard, worship when you're not inspired. Faith means trusting God is at work even when you don't see immediate results.

> *"Let us not become weary in doing good, for at the proper time we will reap a harvest if we do not give up."*
>
> – Galatians 6:9

Faith in Action: Encourage someone this week who might be struggling in their faith. A simple act of encouragement can deeply impact someone else's journey.

Faith When Life Is Hard

Being a Christian doesn't mean you'll avoid struggles. Jesus said challenges would come, but He also promised victory:

> *"In this world you will have trouble. But take heart!*
> *I have overcome the world."* – John 16:33

We often don't know why hardships happen, causing confusion and frustration. Faith helps us trust God even when we don't understand everything going on around us. Even in tough times, God is working something good.

> *"And we know that in all things God works for the good*
> *of those who love him..."* – Romans 8:28

---

❷ DISCUSSION QUESTIONS

1. Can you remember a time you had to trust something you couldn't see?

2. What do you think it means to build your life on God as a foundation?

3. Have you experienced something you knew wasn't just a coincidence?

4. Why do you think faith grows gradually instead of happening instantly?

5. How can you show faith in small ways daily?

▶ ACTION CHALLENGE

Find a moment this week when you clearly notice God at work—write it down. Noticing God's presence helps build your faith over time.

💬 FINAL THOUGHTS

Faith means trusting God even when life doesn't make sense. It's believing He loves you deeply and knows what's best, even in difficult moments. Faith grows as you continually seek God and rely on His promises. Even though life is not always perfect, we know that having faith in Jesus means we will have a perfect eternity with Him.

No matter how you feel, remember that God's love and presence are constant. Keep choosing to trust, knowing He is guiding every step.

🙏 CLOSING PRAYER

"Dear God, help me to trust You more every day. Remind me that You are always with me, especially when things get tough. Thank You for loving me no matter what. Guide me as I grow in faith, and let my life reflect my trust in You. Amen."

CHAPTER 2

Trust

> "Trust in the Lord with all your heart and lean not
> on your own understanding; in all your ways submit
> to him, and he will make your paths straight."
>
> – Proverbs 3:5–6

Before you can fully live out your purpose or respond to God's calling on your life, you need to trust Him. Trust builds directly on the foundation of faith. Once you believe in who God is, trust is what allows you to lean into that belief, even when life is uncertain.

It's one thing to believe God exists—it's another to place your confidence in Him, especially when things don't go as planned. Trust is the bridge between believing in God and actually walking with Him each day. Without it, your actions may become hesitant or unsure. But when trust is strong, you're more willing to take bold steps forward, knowing the One leading you is good, faithful, and wise.

Trust is believing that someone will do what they say they will do. When it comes to God, trust means believing that He is good, He loves you, and He's always working for your best interest—even when you can't see how. Trust means putting your confidence in His will, even when it doesn't line up with what you want or what you think would be best.

Trust isn't always easy. It's natural to want to be in control or to look for answers right away. But trust calls us to rest in the truth that God sees the whole picture and He knows what's ahead. When we trust Him, we choose to follow His lead instead of relying only on what we think or feel.

Why Trust Matters

Trust is the foundation of every strong relationship. Without it, friendships and families start to fall apart. The same is true for your relationship with God. Trust keeps you connected to Him, even in the middle of hard times. It helps you move forward when you're uncertain and gives you peace when things feel out of control.

Trust also impacts how others see you. When you're trust-worthy—when you keep your promises, tell the truth, and take responsibility—people learn they can count on you. Just like you learn to trust God by His faithfulness, others learn to trust you by your actions.

> *"You will keep in perfect peace those whose minds are steadfast, because they trust in you. Trust in the Lord forever, for the Lord, the Lord himself is the Rock eternal."* – Isaiah 26:3-4

For Example...

Imagine you promised a friend you'd help them with something important. But when the time comes, you back out without a good reason. That friend might start to wonder if they can rely on you in the future. On the other hand, if you show up, follow through, and are honest when you make mistakes, you build trust that can last a lifetime.

Or think about how you feel when someone listens to you, keeps your secrets, and stands up for you. It makes you feel safe and valued. That's the power of trust—and it's something we all want in our relationships.

Trust Takes Time

In any relationship, trust grows over time. You build trust with people by watching how they act, how they treat you, and whether they keep their word. The same goes for your relationship with God. As you spend time with Him, read His Word, and see how He's been faithful in your life (and in others'), your trust in Him deepens.

There will be times when you don't understand what God is doing. There may be moments when you feel confused, disappointed, afraid, or even angry. But even then, you can remind yourself of the times God came through before— and trust that He's not finished with your story.

When trust has been built over time, it becomes a steady anchor in uncertain moments. In the beginning of a rela- tionship—whether with God or with people—challenges can shake you because you haven't yet seen how things will turn out. But as trust grows and is reinforced through consistent love, faithfulness, and follow-through, you start to develop confidence that even when things go wrong, they won't fall apart completely.

A setback or disappointment doesn't send you spiraling, because you've already seen how God works things together for good. You've seen people in your life come through

11

before, so with trust, you will be more likely to give them the benefit of the doubt and believe they will again. That kind of trust brings peace in the middle of storms, because you know you're not alone and you know someone has your back.

"When I am afraid, I put my trust in you." – Psalm 56:3

Trusting When It's Hard

This brings the natural transition of understanding that sometimes, trust is easy—like when everything's going well and life feels smooth. But real trust shows up when things don't go your way. Maybe a prayer doesn't get answered the way you hoped, or something happens that leaves you feeling hurt or confused.

In those moments, trusting God means remembering who He is: faithful, loving, and always present. It's okay to have questions. It's okay to feel sad or unsure. But even in that, you can say, *"God, I don't understand, but I still trust You."*

Trusting God when it's hard doesn't make the pain go away, but it brings peace. It reminds you that you're not alone, and that God is working in ways you may not see yet.

"Blessed is the one who trusts in the Lord, whose confidence is in him." – Jeremiah 17:7

Breakout Points

Quick Takeaway: Trust means believing that God is good and faithful, even when life doesn't make sense.

Faith in Action: Think of one area in your life where it's hard to trust God. Pray about it, and ask Him to help you let go and trust Him more.

Think About This: What helps you feel safe enough to trust someone? How can you become a person others can trust?

Did You Know? The Bible uses the word "trust" over 100 times to remind us that God is worthy of our confidence—again and again.

❷ DISCUSSION QUESTIONS

1. What does it mean to trust God with your whole heart?

2. Can you think of a time when trusting God helped you through something difficult?

3. Why is it sometimes hard to trust others or even trust God?

4. What are some ways you can show others that you're a trustworthy person?

5. How do you build trust with someone over time?

⏵ ACTION CHALLENGE

Choose one person this week—maybe a family member, friend, or teacher—and focus on being someone they can trust. Keep your word, be honest, and look for ways to show them you care.

💬 FINAL THOUGHTS

Trust is one of the most powerful parts of any relationship—especially your relationship with God. It's not always easy, and it takes time, but every step you take to trust Him more will draw you closer to His heart.

And just like God wants you to trust Him, He also wants you to be someone others can trust. When you live with honesty, consistency, and love, your life becomes a reflection of His faithfulness.

🙏 CLOSING PRAYER

"Dear God, thank You for being trustworthy and faithful. Help me to trust You more, especially when I don't understand what's happening. Teach me to be someone others can count on, and let my life show Your love and reliability. Amen."

CHAPTER 3

Obedience

"If you love me, keep my commands."

– John 14:15

Once your life is built on a foundation of faith and strengthened by trust, the next step is choosing to respond to that belief with action. Obedience is where your faith becomes visible—it's how trust moves from something you feel to something you live out. You believe in who God is (faith), you rely on His goodness and timing (trust), and now you respond by following His guidance, especially when it's not easy or convenient.

Obedience means choosing to follow instructions from those in positions of authority—with God being the highest authority. It's not just about doing what you're told, but about doing it with the right heart and attitude. Obedience shows that you are willing to listen, trust, and respond with action.

Obedience is the natural outflow of a heart that believes and trusts—and it's a vital part of growing closer to God. In our relationship with Him, obedience is a way we show our love and faith. It's trusting that His commands are not meant to limit us, but to protect and guide us. When we follow what He says, even when it's hard, we grow closer to Him and learn to live in a way that honors Him.

Why Obedience Matters

Obedience builds trust, respect, and discipline. It helps create order in our families, schools, and communities. But most importantly, it deepens our walk with God. When we obey Him, we're saying, *"I trust You more than I trust my own understanding."*

Obedience isn't about being perfect, either—it's about being willing. God knows we'll make mistakes, but He also sees our hearts. When we genuinely try to follow Him, He gives us grace, wisdom, and strength. Acknowledging our flaws lets us embrace God's perfection. This is another amazing way that we can grow in our relationship with Him.

Obedience also opens the door to blessings that we might otherwise miss. Throughout the Bible, God honors those who listen to His voice and follow His commands—not because He wants to control us, but because He wants what's best for us.

When we obey, we align ourselves with His wisdom and protection. It doesn't mean life will be perfect, but it does mean we're walking in step with the One who sees the whole picture. Sometimes the reward is peace, sometimes it's clarity or growth—but there's always blessings in choosing God's way.

> *"Blessed are all who fear the Lord, who walk in obedience to him."* – Psalm 128:1

For Example...

Imagine your parents ask you to help clean up around your house or apartment, or take care of a sibling when they're busy. Obedience means saying "yes"—not just because you're told to, but because you're part of the family, and families work together. When you choose to help without complaining, you're not just doing a chore—you're strengthening your place in the family and contributing to something bigger than yourself.

Obedience like that brings peace, unity, and joy to the home. It reminds you that with responsibility also comes the blessing of being trusted, valued, and deeply connected. And just like obedience in your family leads to shared blessings, obedience to God brings you closer to Him and invites His goodness into your life.

Obedience with Discernment

Obedience is important—but it should never be blind. There may be times when someone in authority asks you to do something that feels wrong, makes you uncomfortable, or goes against what you know God says is right. In those situations, obedience should take a back seat to wisdom.

God calls us to be respectful, but also to think, ask questions, and use discernment. If a friend, family member, or any adult tells you to do something that doesn't sit right in your spirit, it's okay to pause and say "no." True obedience never means going along with something that could harm you or others. Your first loyalty is always to God and His truth.

> *"Peter and the other apostles replied: 'We must obey God rather than human beings!'"* – Acts 5:29

Obedience Grows Our Faith

Every time we obey—even in small ways—we grow stronger in our faith. Obedience builds habits that shape our hearts. It helps us become more aware of God's voice and more willing to follow where He leads.

Obedience also ties back to trust. Sometimes we have to say "no" to what we want in the moment, so we can say "yes" to what God wants for our future. And even when the path doesn't make sense in the moment, trust reminds us that God's way is always better. But we can't truly trust someone we don't believe in—this is why obedience must be built on both faith and trust.

Faith gives us the foundation to believe that God exists and that He is good. Trust helps us rely on Him, even when we can't see the full picture. Once that trust is in place, obedience becomes the natural next step. It's the action that flows from believing and trusting. When we obey God, we're saying, *"I believe You, I trust You, and I'm willing to follow You."* Obedience is the visible expression of our inward faith.

"Whoever has my commands and keeps them is the one who loves me." – John 14:21

Breakout Points

Quick Takeaway: Obedience is doing what's right—even when it's hard—because you trust God and want to follow Him.

Faith in Action: Think of one thing you've been putting off that you know God wants you to do. Make a plan to do it sooner rather than later.

Think About This: Is there ever a time when it's okay to say "no" to authority? What does God's Word say about that?

Did You Know? Jesus was obedient to God all the way to the cross—not because it was easy, but because He loved and trusted His Father completely.

❓ DISCUSSION QUESTIONS

1. What does obedience mean to you?

2. Can you think of a time when you obeyed even though it was hard?

3. Why is it important to obey God even when we don't understand everything?

4. How can you know when to say "no" to something that feels wrong?

5. How does obedience help strengthen your faith?

⏵ ACTION CHALLENGE

Pick one area where you've struggled with obedience—at home, in school, or in your relationship with God. Ask for His help, and take one small step this week to do what's right, even if it's difficult.

💬 FINAL THOUGHTS

Obedience isn't just about rules—it's about trust, love, and surrender. When you obey God, you're saying, *"I believe Your way is best."* And when you use wisdom and courage to say "no" to things that don't align with His truth, you're showing strength and discernment.

God isn't looking for perfection—He's looking for hearts that are willing to listen and follow. When you live with that kind of obedience, you'll grow in faith, strength, and wisdom.

🙏 CLOSING PRAYER

"Dear God, help me to obey You with a willing heart. Teach me to listen to Your voice and to follow Your ways, even when it's hard. Give me wisdom to know when something isn't right, and courage to stand for Your truth. Thank You for Your love and patience as I learn to trust and follow You. Amen."

CHAPTER 4

Conviction

"Be on your guard; stand firm in the faith; be courageous; be strong."

– 1 Corinthians 16:13

After learning about faith, trust, and obedience, the next step is developing the strength to stand firm in those beliefs—this is where conviction comes in. Conviction means having a strong belief in what is right and staying true to those beliefs, no matter how difficult it may be. It is the inner strength that helps you stand firm in your values, especially when others around you are going in a different direction.

Conviction is more than just having an opinion—it's about being deeply rooted in what you know is true and right, especially based on God's Word. When you have conviction, you aren't easily swayed by peer pressure, popular opinions, or fear of being different. Instead, you hold tight to what is good, even if it makes you stand out. It helps shape your identity and builds confidence that comes from knowing you are living with purpose.

Why Conviction is Important

Conviction plays a major role in how you live out your faith and your values. Without conviction, it becomes easy to give in to the opinions and demands of others when life gets uncomfortable or when others challenge your beliefs. Conviction gives you strength to stand firm on your foundation of faith when you're unsure or when you're tempted to follow the crowd.

It also shows others that your faith and values aren't just words—they are part of who you are. People will notice when you make hard choices for the right reasons. They may not always agree with you, but they will respect you for your conviction.

> *"If anyone, then, knows the good they ought to do and doesn't do it, it is sin for them."* – James 4:17

For Example...

Imagine you're with your friends and they start making fun of someone else. Deep down, you know it's wrong, but everyone is laughing and going along with it. Conviction is that feeling in your heart that tells you, *"This isn't right."* And if you choose to speak up or walk away, you're standing on your convictions—even if it means being left out.

Or maybe you're tempted to cheat on a test because everyone else is doing it and you don't want to fall behind. Conviction is what keeps you honest. It's that quiet strength that reminds you who you are and who you want to be.

Conviction Requires Courage and Wisdom

Preparing to stand on your convictions starts before you're ever tested. You can get ready by knowing what you believe, why you believe it, and staying connected to God through prayer and reading Scripture. When you've thought through your values ahead of time, it becomes easier to stand firm when pressure comes.

It's like putting on armor before heading into battle—you won't be caught off guard when the challenge hits. Be clear about what matters most to you, and ask God to give you strength in those moments when it's hard to stand alone.

Similar to what you learned in the last chapter, it's important to remember that conviction doesn't mean being stubborn or refusing to listen. It means holding onto what you believe is right, but also having the humility to learn and grow. Sometimes, we realize that something we believed in strongly wasn't actually true, or it wasn't based on God's truth. When that happens, real conviction allows us to admit we were wrong and change course.

God doesn't call us to stay blindly loyal to our opinions. He calls us to stand on His truth. That means our convictions should always be open to reflection and correction. If what you believe is truly right, it will stand up to questions. You should never be afraid to ask, explore, and make sure your convictions line up with God's Word.

> *"The way of fools seems right to them, but the wise listen to advice."* – Proverbs 12:15

Conviction Inspires Through Kindness

Your convictions don't just shape who you are—they influence those around you. When you stand firm in your beliefs, especially during difficult moments, you set an example that can encourage and strengthen others. People naturally notice when you stay true to what's right, and your actions often speak louder than your words.

But how you communicate those convictions matters deeply. It's possible to be firm without being harsh. The Bible tells us to speak the truth in love (Ephesians 4:15). That means holding on to your values with kindness, humility, and respect. If someone challenges your beliefs or asks questions, responding with patience and understanding shows real strength. It demonstrates that conviction isn't just about proving others wrong—it's about reflecting God's truth with genuine care.

When you express your convictions gently but confidently, you show people that truth and kindness can coexist. Your family, friends, and peers may not always agree immediately, but your respectful approach plants seeds that can grow into deeper conversations and even changed hearts.

You will never change someone's mind or heart by demanding it or yelling at them. Through demonstration and talking with others respectfully, you allow them to come to the conclusion on their own. This is how God changes minds and hearts.

> *"A gentle answer turns away wrath, but a harsh word stirs up anger."* – Proverbs 15:1

Remember, your conviction is powerful not only because of what you say, but because of how you say it and live it out. When others see you consistently choose kindness and integrity, they feel encouraged to do the same. In this way, your conviction doesn't just define your own life; it inspires others to build stronger character and faith as well.

Breakout Points

Quick Takeaway: Conviction is standing firm in what you know is right, even when it's hard or unpopular.

Faith in Action: The next time you're pressured to go along with something you know is wrong, pause and ask, *"What does God say about this?"*

Think About This: Are your convictions based on truth or just what you've always heard? Have you taken time to examine them?

Did You Know? The word "conviction" comes from a Latin word meaning "to prove or show." A strong conviction is something that has been tested and proven to be true.

❓ DISCUSSION QUESTIONS

1. Can you think of a time when you stood up for something you believed in, even though it was hard?

2. Why do you think it's important not to let other people decide what your values should be?

3. What makes a belief strong enough to turn into a conviction?

4. How can you tell if your convictions are based on truth or opinion?

5. Why is it important to stay open to correction, even when you feel strongly about something?

⏵ ACTION CHALLENGE

Think of one value or belief you hold that really matters to you. This week, write down why it matters and where it comes from. Then look for one opportunity to live it out.

💬 FINAL THOUGHTS

Conviction gives you the strength to stand tall when everything around you is pushing you to blend in. It helps you live with purpose and clarity, knowing that you're not just following the crowd—you're following God. It may not always be easy, but it will always be worth it.

Being a person of conviction doesn't mean you never change your mind. It means you're committed to living by the truth and willing to grow. God honors those who seek wisdom and walk in His ways. Let your convictions be built on His Word, and you will never be without a firm place to stand.

🙏 CLOSING PRAYER

"Dear God, help me to be a person of conviction. Give me the courage to stand for what is right and the wisdom to grow when I need to learn. Keep me grounded in Your Word so that my values reflect Your truth. Help me to live boldly, even when it's hard. Amen."

CHAPTER 5

Courage

"Have I not commanded you? Be strong and courageous. Do not be afraid; do not be discouraged, for the Lord your God will be with you wherever you go."

– Joshua 1:9

There will be times in life when doing what's right won't feel easy—and that's exactly when courage matters most. Courage isn't something that only shows up in emergencies or big, dramatic moments. It grows in everyday choices: the quiet ones, the difficult ones, and especially the ones that stretch your faith.

It's easy to live life without challenges or having to make difficult decisions. True courage is found in the moments when you choose the narrow path, the harder choice, or the unpopular stance because you know it honors God. While the world may applaud comfort and compromise, God calls us to something better—and braver.

"Enter through the narrow gate. For wide is the gate and broad is the road that leads to destruction, and many

enter through it. But small is the gate and narrow is the road that leads to life, and only a few find it."

– Matthew 7:13-14

Courage means doing what's right, especially when it's scary or uncomfortable. The truth is, fear and doubt are normal. But courage reminds us that even when we're unsure, we can still move forward with hope and strength—because we trust that God is with us every step of the way. This is how He builds trust with us, which will increase our conviction.

Courage is choosing to move forward even when fear is whispering in your ear. It's not about being fearless—it's about doing the right thing even when you're afraid. You can be courageous and fearful at the same time! God gives us strength to be courageous when we trust in Him and rely on His presence.

Courage Comes in All Forms

Courage isn't always loud or dramatic. We often picture bravery as something that happens on a battlefield or during a rescue, but most courage shows up in much smaller moments. It's choosing to get out of bed on a really hard day. It's raising your hand in class when you're nervous, or telling the truth when lying would be easier. It's being yourself, even when you feel different from everyone else.

Courage also shows up when you choose to act for someone else's good. It might mean standing up for someone who's being picked on, choosing kindness when you're angry, or inviting someone into a group who's usually left out. Sometimes, it's walking alongside someone who's hurting, even when you don't know what to say. And on other days, courage is simply showing up, trying again, or facing one more challenge with faith.

No act of courage is too small for God to notice. The world might overlook quiet bravery, but God sees the strength it takes to keep going, to do what's right, and to care for others. Every time you act with courage—whether anyone sees it or not—you're building a stronger, more faithful character.

> *"Be on your guard; stand firm in the faith; be courageous; be strong."* – 1 Corinthians 16:13

Why Courage Matters

Courage helps us grow, take healthy risks, and step into the calling God has for us. It pushes us to trust Him more deeply. When we avoid things because they're hard or scary, we miss out on the blessings that can come from obedience.

Courage also inspires others. When you stand up for what's right or push through something difficult, it shows people around you that they can do the same. Courage is contagious and when you lean on God, He gives you everything you need to take that next step.

Courage also teaches us to rely less on our own strength and more on God's. When we take a step forward, even though we feel unsure or afraid, we're reminded that bravery doesn't come from having it all together—it comes from trusting that God will meet us in the unknown. That kind of courage builds resilience and deepens our faith. It prepares our hearts for those everyday moments when we need to speak up, show up, or stand firm in our beliefs—even when no one else does.

For Example...

Imagine you're the only one in your friend group who doesn't want to go along with a joke that's hurtful. It takes courage to speak up or walk away. Or maybe you're dealing with anxiety or sadness, and no one knows. Just facing the day and doing your best is a quiet, yet powerful kind of courage.

Maybe you're afraid to try something new because you don't want to fail. Courage says, *"I may be nervous and I might not be successful the first time, but I'm going to try anyway."* God doesn't ask us to be perfect—He asks us to trust Him as we take one step at a time.

Courage Is Rooted in Faith

You don't have to find courage all on your own. Real courage comes from knowing God is with you. He promises to never leave you or forsake you, no matter what you're facing. When you feel weak or afraid, you can pray for strength.

God has helped people show courage throughout the Bible—like David facing Goliath, Esther standing before the king, or Daniel in the lion's den. In each story, the courage didn't come from being fearless. It came from trusting God more than giving in to the fear.

One of the most powerful ways we can show courage through our faith is by encouraging others in theirs. It takes bravery to speak about your beliefs, especially when you're not sure how others will respond. Whether you're sharing the gospel with someone new or talking about your faith with friends, you're planting seeds of hope or watering the seeds God has already planted. These moments may feel small, but they can make a big difference in someone's life—and yours.

"When I am afraid, I put my trust in you." – Psalm 56:3

Breakout Points

Quick Takeaway: Courage isn't the absence of fear—it's choosing to do what's right, even when you're afraid.

Faith in Action: Think of one small, brave step you can take today. It could be speaking up, trying something new, or asking for help.

Think About This: When was the last time you showed courage in a quiet way?

Did You Know? Many people in the Bible showed courage not through power, but through obedience, prayer, and quiet faith.

❓ DISCUSSION QUESTIONS

1. What does courage look like in your everyday life?

2. Can you think of a time when you had to be brave, even if it didn't feel like a big moment?

3. Why do you think it's important to show courage, even when no one notices?

4. How does knowing God is with you help you face your fears?

5. What is one fear you can ask God to help you overcome this week?

▶ ACTION CHALLENGE

This week, do one thing that takes courage—big or small. It could be standing up for someone, admitting a mistake, or simply showing up and giving your best. Write down how it made you feel afterward.

💬 FINAL THOUGHTS

Courage doesn't always roar. Sometimes, it's a whisper that says, *"I'll try again tomorrow."* No act of courage is too small in God's eyes. Whether you're facing something big or just trying to get through the day, choosing to keep going is powerful.

God is always with you, even in the moments that feel scary or overwhelming. He promises to give you strength and He delights in every step of bravery you take.

🙏 CLOSING PRAYER

"Dear God, thank You for always being with me. When I feel afraid or uncertain, help me to trust in You. Give me the courage to do what's right—even when it's hard—and remind me that every small act of bravery matters to You. Amen."

CHAPTER 6

Integrity

"The integrity of the upright guides them, but the unfaithful are destroyed by their duplicity."

– Proverbs 11:3

Integrity means choosing honesty and consistency in your actions, even when no one is watching. It means being the same person privately as you are publicly. Integrity is doing what's right simply because it's right—not just because someone is watching or you'll get rewarded.

Having integrity means making choices that align with your faith. It's easy to say you believe in God, but integrity means your actions will reflect your belief, no matter the situation. God always sees your choices—even the hidden ones—and integrity means living in a way that honors Him at all times.

If your integrity is weak or questionable, it affects how people view every other aspect of your character. Without integrity, even your best qualities may be doubted or over-looked. Strong integrity, however, acts as proof of your faith and serves as the foundation upon which all other virtues stand.

"Whoever walks in integrity walks securely, but whoever takes crooked paths will be found out." – Proverbs 10:9

Integrity Matters

Since your integrity impacts how others perceive you, it directly shapes their ability to trust you. When people see you consistently choosing honesty, even in small matters, they will respect you and rely on you more. But if you often bend the truth or take shortcuts, people start to question everything you say or do. Integrity builds credibility.

Integrity also strengthens your character. The more you practice it, the more natural it becomes. Integrity makes your faith genuine, strong, and lasting—helping you grow in other areas like accountability, trust, and respect.

Integrity doesn't mean you never mess up. Everyone makes mistakes, but integrity is about how you respond. It means admitting when you're wrong, apologizing sincerely, and learning from the experience. Integrity is about continual growth, honesty, and humility.

Living with integrity isn't always easy. That's why the character qualities you've already learned—like conviction and courage—play a big role. Conviction gives you a clear sense of right and wrong, and courage gives you the strength to act on that conviction, even when it's uncomfortable or unpopular. Integrity depends on both. The more you build those qualities, the easier it becomes to stand firm in your actions and stay true to your values.

For Example...

Imagine you're walking home and find a wallet full of cash on the sidewalk. Nobody is around to see. You have two choices: keep the money or find the owner.

Integrity asks, *"What's the right thing to do?"* Even if no one would know, you would know and God would, too. That little voice in the back of your head, telling you to do the right thing is the Holy Spirit. This is how God convicts you to do the right thing. Integrity leads you to return the wallet—not because you have to, but because it's right.

Integrity Around You

Integrity isn't just for people. Think about bridges or airplanes. Engineers regularly inspect them to ensure safety. If they discover even tiny cracks or flaws, they repair them immediately. If they ignored those flaws, the results could be disastrous.

Just like buildings or airplanes need integrity to be reliable, your life needs integrity to be trustworthy. Even small lies or hidden dishonesty can weaken your character. Eventually, your true self always shows.

> *"The Lord detests lying lips, but he delights in people who are trustworthy."* – Proverbs 12:22

Integrity Under Pressure

It's easy to make good choices when life is going smoothly or when others are watching. But true integrity is revealed when things get tough—when you're tired, scared, tempted, or facing significant pressure. Integrity means holding firm to your values, even when it would be easier or more convenient not to.

The Bible gives us powerful examples of people who demonstrated integrity under great pressure. One of the best examples is Joseph, who was sold into slavery by his brothers. Even when falsely accused and thrown into prison, Joseph chose integrity. He never gave in to bitterness or took shortcuts to freedom.

Instead, he consistently did what was right, trusting God even in terrible circumstances. Eventually, Joseph's unwavering integrity led to his rise as second-in-command in Egypt, allowing him to save countless lives, including his brothers' who had wronged him.

> "In everything set them an example by doing what is good. In your teaching show integrity, seriousness and soundness of speech that cannot be condemned."
>
> – Titus 2:7–8

Integrity under pressure doesn't always have such dramatic outcomes, but it always matters deeply to God. Imagine you're pressured by friends or peers to do something you know is wrong. On one hand, it's easier to just give in because the people pressuring you won't give you a hard time. But when you stand firm, even if it means facing criticism or feeling left out, your character grows stronger. Your integrity becomes clearer and your faith deeper.

Pressure isn't pleasant, but it has a purpose. Just as gold becomes purer when refined in fire, our character is purified and strengthened when tested by difficult circumstances. Each decision to remain honest, loyal, and faithful under pressure not only honors God, but it shapes you into the person He created you to be.

When you're feeling tempted to compromise your integrity, pause and pray. Ask God for strength and clarity. Choosing integrity in moments of pressure won't always be easy, but it will always be worth it.

> *"Consider it pure joy, my brothers and sisters, whenever you face trials of many kinds, because you know that the testing of your faith produces perseverance."*

– James 1:2–3

Breakout Points

Quick Takeaway: Integrity is choosing to do the right thing, even when no one is watching.

Faith in Action: Next time you're faced with a decision between honesty and dishonesty, pause and think: "Would I make this choice if someone was watching me?"

Think About This: Would you rather be someone people respect for your honesty, or someone people doubt because they can't trust your word?

Did You Know? The word "integrity" comes from the Latin word integer, meaning "whole" or "complete." Integrity means being the same person everywhere— not one way with family and another with friends.

❷ DISCUSSION QUESTIONS

1. Why is it important to be honest even if no one will ever know?

2. Can you remember a time when you had to choose between doing the right thing and taking an easier path? How did it feel afterward?

3. Why does integrity matter in your friendships?

4. How does having integrity in small things help you make better choices in big decisions?

5. How does knowing that God sees everything influence your choices?

⏵ ACTION CHALLENGE

Find at least one situation this week to practice integrity—maybe it's admitting a mistake, telling the truth when it's difficult, or returning something that's not yours. Be sure to take notice how you feel afterward.

💬 FINAL THOUGHTS

Dishonesty is common today, but it always brings consequences. Lies damage trust and relationships, and even small lies can quickly escalate. Integrity protects your character and reputation.

Remember, dishonesty began when Satan lied to Adam and Eve in the Garden of Eden. That lie led to sin, pain, and separation from God, impacting every human since.

Choosing honesty helps restore trust and strengthens your connection with God and others.

Integrity is crucial because it touches every aspect of your life. It's not always easy to choose honesty, but it's always worth it. A life built on integrity is stable, strong, and respected.

🙏 CLOSING PRAYER

"Dear God, help me live with integrity. Teach me to choose honesty even when no one else is watching. Guide my words and actions to reflect truth and kindness. Help me to grow into someone others trust, and most importantly, someone who honors You in everything I do. Amen."

CHAPTER 7

Self-Discipline

"No discipline seems pleasant at the time, but painful. Later on, however, it produces a harvest of righteousness and peace for those who have been trained by it."

– Hebrews 12:11

Self-discipline is one of the most important tools for turning good intentions into lasting growth. It helps you stay focused on what matters, even when distractions or emotions try to pull you in other directions. Even the strongest believers face distractions—what matters most is that you keep trying and trust God to help you grow.

Whether you're working toward a goal, resisting temptation, or building healthy habits, self-discipline is what helps you follow through—especially when things get hard. As your faith deepens and your character grows, learning to manage your choices with wisdom and strength becomes a vital part of becoming the person God designed you to be.

Self-discipline means making choices that help you grow, even when they're not easy or fun. It's about controlling your actions, thoughts, and words instead of letting your feelings or habits control you. When you practice self-discipline, you choose what's right over what's easy.

The word "discipline" comes from the same root as "disciple," which means a learner or follower. So when we talk about discipline, we're not talking about punishment—we're talking about learning and growth. Self-discipline is how we train ourselves to become the people God created us to be.

Why Self-Discipline Matters

Self-discipline helps you stay on track with your goals, your values, and your faith. It gives you the strength to say "no" to things that could lead you away from God, and "yes" to things that help you grow closer to Him. Without self-discipline, it's easy to fall into bad habits or give in to temptation. But when you choose to stay focused, you build strength, character, and a deeper relationship with God.

Self-discipline also helps you become someone others can depend on, as was mentioned in the last chapter. When you consistently follow through on your responsibilities—at home, at school, or in your relationships—you show that your words and actions can be trusted. This kind of reliability doesn't just build your own character; it builds respect from others and opens the door for greater opportunities to lead, serve, and influence in meaningful ways.

Finally, self-discipline gives you something many people don't expect: freedom. When you learn to set healthy limits and take control of your choices, you gain the freedom to pursue the things that matter most—without being constantly distracted or controlled by impulse. Instead of living reactively, you begin living with direction and purpose. Over time, this kind of freedom leads to peace of mind, better relationships, and a stronger sense of joy in knowing you're honoring God with the way you live.

"Like a city whose walls are broken through is a person who lacks self-control." – Proverbs 25:28

For Example...

Imagine you have homework to do, but you'd rather play video games or scroll through your phone. Self-discipline helps you choose to finish your work first, even when it's not what you feel like doing.

Or maybe someone says something unkind, and you feel like snapping back. Self-discipline reminds you to pause, take a breath, and respond with kindness instead. It's those small moments of control that add up to a strong, wise, and faithful life.

On the other hand, someone who lacks self-discipline may constantly put off important tasks, speak without thinking, or give in to bad habits again and again. Over time, this kind of carelessness can lead to broken trust, missed opportunities, unnecessary stress, and most of all, regret. Without self-discipline, it becomes harder to stay focused on what really matters and easier to drift away from the path God has laid out for you.

Self-Discipline Grows Over Time

No one is born with self-discipline—it's something we learn and strengthen as we grow. And just like exercising a muscle, the more you practice, the stronger it gets. Every time you make a wise choice, even when it's tough, you're building the kind of life God wants for you.

It's also important to be patient with yourself. You won't always get it right, and that's okay. God isn't asking for perfection—He's asking for a willing heart. Every step you take in the right direction matters.

As you continue practicing self-discipline, it often becomes easier—because you begin to notice how it leads to peace, progress, and less stress. Taking care of responsibilities instead of putting them off helps your future self avoid unnecessary pressure. Over time, those positive results make it more natural to keep choosing what's wise and right.

Whether it's finishing homework, making time to pray, or choosing honesty in a tough moment, self-discipline helps you avoid regret and stay on track. It's how we stop "kicking the can down the road" and start building a life that honors God and reflects strong character.

> *"For the Spirit God gave us does not make us timid, but gives us power, love and self-discipline."*
>
> – 2 Timothy 1:7

Breakout Points

Quick Takeaway: Self-discipline means choosing what's right over what's easy, even when it's hard.

Faith in Action: Think of one area where you want to grow in self-discipline—like your words, your time, or your attitude—and ask God to help you take one small step this week.

Think About This: What does it mean to train yourself like a disciple? How is that different from just following rules?

Did You Know? One of the greatest examples of self-discipline in the Bible is when Jesus fasted for 40 days and 40 nights in the wilderness. Even though He was tired and hungry, He resisted every temptation the devil threw at Him. Instead of giving in, Jesus responded with truth from Scripture. You can read about this powerful moment in Matthew 4:1–11.

❓ DISCUSSION QUESTIONS

1. What's one area of your life where it's hard to stay disciplined?

2. How does self-discipline help you follow God more closely?

3. Can you think of a time when making the harder choice helped you grow?

4. Why do you think God values self-discipline so much?

5. What can you do when you mess up or give in to temptation?

▶ ACTION CHALLENGE

Pick one habit or area where you want to grow in self-discipline. Make a plan to work on it for the next seven days. Ask someone you trust to encourage you and help you stay on track.

💬 FINAL THOUGHTS

Self-discipline isn't about being perfect—it's about being consistent. It's choosing to do what's right, even when it's difficult or inconvenient. Every time you practice it, you're building strength—not just in your habits, but in your heart.

God knows it's not always easy. But He sees every small step you take and honors your desire to grow. Self-discipline helps you become the person He created you to be—someone who is faithful, focused, and dependable.

And remember, this isn't something you master overnight. Self-discipline is a lifelong journey. The small choices you make now—the quiet moments when you choose to follow through—are shaping your future in powerful ways. You're not just building better habits; you're building a life that honors God and reflects His character.

CLOSING PRAYER

"Dear God, thank you for loving me even when I fall short. Help me to grow in self-discipline so I can make choices that honor You. Give me strength to stay focused, courage to keep trying, and a heart that wants to grow. Amen."

CHAPTER 8

Resilience

> "Let us not become weary in doing good, for at the proper time we will reap a harvest if we do not give up."
>
> – Galatians 6:9

Sometimes life knocks the wind out of you. Maybe it's a sudden change, a hard loss, or just a stretch of days that feels too heavy to carry. That's when resilience becomes more than just a word—it becomes a lifeline. Resilience is the inner strength that compels you to get back up, even when it would be easier to give up. And while it doesn't erase the struggle, it gives you the strength to walk through it without losing hope.

Resilience means *choosing* to get back up when life knocks you down. It's the choice to push through when things are hard, the courage to try again after failure, and the faith to believe that God is still at work—even when you feel weak or tired. Resilience doesn't mean you never feel discouraged. It means you don't let discouragement stop you.

Everyone faces challenges—disappointment, failure, rejection, loss. Resilience is the determination to press forward, trusting that God will give you the strength you need for each new step. It's not about being *perfect*; it's about being *consistent*.

Why Resilience Matters

Life will bring ups and downs. Some days will be fun and full of success, while others will feel frustrating or unfair. Resilience helps you navigate both. It gives you the ability to bounce back after something goes wrong and to keep doing the right thing, even when it's difficult.

Resilience builds maturity, character, and confidence. When you learn to keep going—when you don't give up— you become stronger inside and out. And that strength comes from God, who promises to walk with you through every storm.

Resilience also helps you stay grounded when your emotions are strong and circumstances are confusing. It teaches you to pause, breathe, and keep your focus on what you know is true—even when you don't feel strong in the moment. That kind of calm determination can only grow when you've faced adversity and keep your resolve. The more you practice resilience, the more confidence you'll have when challenges come again.

> "The Lord gives strength to his people; the Lord blesses his people with peace." – Psalm 29:11

For Example...

Imagine you studied really hard for a test but still didn't get the grade you hoped for. Resilience means learning from what went wrong, asking for help if needed, and trying again next time without giving up.

Or maybe you tried out for a team, a part in a play, or a position in student council and didn't make it. Resilience is what helps you say, *"That was tough, but I'm going to keep trying, keep growing, and keep believing God has a plan for me."*

Resilience and Disappointment

People who never face failure, distress, or loss are often unable to develop true resilience. If everything always comes easy, it's difficult to learn how to cope when life gets hard. But facing challenges gives us the chance to grow stronger, wiser, and more dependent on God.

Resilience is extremely important when we face disappointment. It's normal to feel upset when things don't go our way, but those moments can also be opportunities for growth. They remind us that success isn't about always winning—it's about how we respond when things are hard.

You're probably familiar with the saying, "It's not how many times you get knocked down, it's how many times you get back up." No one expects you to enjoy adversity, but you can learn to grow from it. So when difficulties come your way, don't see them as setbacks. See them as opportunities to build the kind of strength that lasts.

Even Jesus faced rejection and pain, but He never gave up. His resilience was powered by His relationship with the Father and His purpose. When you stay close to God, He'll give you the strength to move forward, no matter what you're facing.

> *"We are hard pressed on every side, but not crushed; perplexed, but not in despair... struck down, but not destroyed."* – 2 Corinthians 4:8–9

Resilience and God's Strength

It's important to remember that you don't have to be strong all by yourself. Resilience isn't just about pushing through—it's about leaning on God when you feel tired, discouraged, or overwhelmed. He doesn't expect you to carry the weight of every hardship alone. In fact, one of the most powerful things you can do is admit when you need His help.

> *"God is our refuge and strength, an ever-present help in trouble."* – Psalm 46:1

That verse is a reminder that you're never alone in your struggles. God is always with you, ready to give you the strength, peace, and courage you need to keep going. Every time you turn to Him in your weakness and choose to keep moving forward, your faith grows—and so does your resilience.

Breakout Points

Quick Takeaway: Resilience means not giving up—
even when things are tough or don't go your way.

Faith in Action: The next time you face a challenge or
feel discouraged, pause and ask God for strength.

Think About This: What's something hard you've gone
through that made you stronger in the end?

Did You Know? The Bible is filled with resilient people—
like Joseph, who was sold by his brothers, falsely accused,
and thrown in prison before becoming a great leader.

❓ DISCUSSION QUESTIONS

1. What does resilience look like in your life?
2. Can you think of a time when you didn't give up, even though it was hard?
3. How does your faith help you stay strong during tough times?
4. Why do you think God allows us to go through difficult experiences?
5. Who is someone you admire for their resilience? What can you learn from them?

▶ ACTION CHALLENGE

Think of a situation where you're tempted to give up. This week, make a choice to push those negative thoughts out of your head. Pray for strength, ask for support if you need it, and remind yourself that God is with you.

💬 FINAL THOUGHTS

Resilience doesn't mean pretending everything is okay. It means trusting God enough to keep going, even when life feels heavy. It's about showing up, trying again, and believing that He's not finished with your story.

Every time you choose to rise after falling, to press on through frustration, or to trust God in your struggle, you're building resilience—and becoming more like Jesus, who never gave up.

🙏 CLOSING PRAYER

"Dear God, thank You for being with me in every high and low. When I feel weak, give me Your strength. When I feel discouraged, remind me that You're still working. Help me to be resilient and to keep trusting You no matter what. Amen."

CHAPTER 9

Perseverance

> "Let us run with perseverance the race marked out for us, fixing our eyes on Jesus, the pioneer and perfecter of faith."
>
> – Hebrews 12:1b–2a

Perseverance is the quiet strength that helps you keep going when things are difficult, uncertain, or even discouraging. It's more than bouncing back from challenges—it's the action of pressing onward, regardless of how long the road is or how slow progress might be.

This quality builds on resilience. Resilience helps you rise after a knockdown, but perseverance keeps you moving forward one step at a time, even when it's easier to give up. It's what helps you stay faithful in your walk with God, remain committed to your goals, and finish what you've started—even when your motivation fades.

Perseverance isn't just about pushing through hard things. It's about learning to trust that the process itself has value. Every time you stay committed through difficulty, you grow in endurance, patience, and character. And as you do, you'll begin to see how perseverance shapes you into someone stronger, wiser, and more deeply grounded in faith.

Why Perseverance Matters

Perseverance matters because growth takes time. Whether you're learning something new, working toward a goal, or building your faith, meaningful progress rarely happens overnight. Perseverance helps you stay the course through long seasons of waiting, small steps, and unseen progress. Without it, we often give up right before things begin to change.

It also deepens your trust in God. Perseverance gives you the opportunity to rely on Him, not just in moments of crisis, but in the slow, quiet stretches when nothing seems to be happening. In those moments, faith becomes more than belief—it becomes a daily practice of choosing to keep going on days that don't give you immediate results.

Finally, perseverance builds dependability and spiritual maturity. It helps you stick with what you've committed to—your responsibilities, relationships, and values—even when you feel tired or unsure. This kind of steady faithfulness sets a strong example for others and makes you someone who can be trusted with greater things.

"You need to persevere so that when you have done the will of God, you will receive what he has promised."

– Hebrews 10:36

For Example...

Imagine you set a goal to read your Bible every day for a month. At first, you're excited. But after a week, it feels like a chore. Perseverance helps you keep going, not because it's easy, but because it's worth it.

Or maybe you're trying to improve your attitude, but you keep slipping into old habits. Perseverance reminds you that progress is made step by step—and even when you mess up, you can start again.

Waiting with Hope

One of the hardest parts of perseverance is waiting—especially when doubts creep in because you start to question how things will turn out. But when you wait with hope, you're not just sitting still. You're trusting that God is working behind the scenes, even if you don't see it yet. Hope is what gives perseverance its purpose. Without it, we'd have no reason to keep going.

As Christians, our hope isn't just in temporary outcomes—it's in Jesus. We believe that He is coming back to finish what He started 2,000 years ago. That kind of hope goes far beyond wishing—it's a confident expectation rooted in God's promises. Because of what Jesus has already done, we can face each day knowing that the story isn't over yet.

Some of the most faithful people in the Bible had to wait for years—like Noah building the ark or Abraham and Sarah waiting for a child. They didn't always get it right, but they didn't walk away from God. Their stories remind us that God is always on time, even when His timeline is different from ours.

Hope is the fuel that keeps perseverance alive. We persevere because we believe there is more ahead—more healing, more growth, more joy, more of God's goodness. Whether we're hoping for change in a tough situation, strength for the day, or the ultimate restoration of all things through Christ, hope gives us the courage to keep moving forward.

"Let us not become weary in doing good, for at the proper time we will reap a harvest if we do not give up."

– Galatians 6:9

Perseverance Shapes Who You're Becoming

Perseverance doesn't just help you get through something— it helps shape the person you're becoming in the process. Trials, setbacks, and delays often feel like obstacles, but they're also classrooms where some of life's most important lessons are taught. These moments teach us patience, grit, and empathy. They stretch our faith and reveal what we truly believe when things don't go as planned.

God often uses slow and difficult seasons to do His deepest work in us. While we may focus on the finish line, God is shaping our hearts for the journey. He builds humility in our struggles, compassion through our pain, and strength by helping us endure. You may not always feel it happening in the moment, but every time you keep going with a faithful heart, something inside you is being refined.

Anyone who has strong character didn't get there by accident. They've persevered through challenges, learned hard lessons, and grown stronger over time. Perseverance forms the kind of person others can trust—someone who doesn't give up easily, who learns from mistakes, and who stays committed through difficulty. With God's help, you're not just pushing forward—you're being transformed from the inside out.

> *"Consider it pure joy, my brothers and sisters, whenever you face trials of many kinds, because you know that the testing of your faith produces perseverance. Let perseverance finish its work so that you may be mature and complete, not lacking anything."* – James 1:2-4

Breakout Points

Quick Takeaway: Perseverance is the daily choice to stay faithful, even when things are slow or hard.

Faith in Action: This week, commit to something small—like a daily prayer or habit—and stick with it, even when you don't feel like it.

Think About This: What's something you've started that you need to finish? What might God be teaching you through the waiting?

Did You Know? The word "perseverance" comes from Latin roots that mean "to continue through to the end." It's all about steady effort, not instant success.

❓ DISCUSSION QUESTIONS

1. How is perseverance different from resilience?
2. Why is it hard to keep going when you don't see quick results?
3. What helps you stay motivated to do the right thing, even when it's tough?
4. How does perseverance help you grow closer to God?
5. Who is someone in the Bible (or in your life) who shows perseverance?

▶ ACTION CHALLENGE

Pick one area in your life where you feel tempted to give up. Make a plan to stick with it for one more week. Ask God each day to give you strength and focus.

💬 FINAL THOUGHTS

Perseverance isn't always exciting. Sometimes it's simply putting one foot in front of the other, even with no end in sight. But with every step, God is shaping your heart and building your character.

Don't give up just because it's hard or slow. Keep your eyes on Jesus. Keep doing the next right thing. Trust that your faithfulness will bear fruit in time.

🙏 CLOSING PRAYER

"Dear God, help me to keep going, even when I feel tired or discouraged. Give me strength to stay faithful in the small things and to trust Your timing in everything. Thank you for walking with me every step of the way. Amen."

CHAPTER 10

Patience

> "Be still before the Lord and wait patiently for him; do not fret when people succeed in their ways, when they carry out their wicked schemes."
>
> – Psalm 37:7

Patience doesn't come naturally to most of us. It's a lesson that's usually never fun to learn, but is crucial for finding contentment and peace when life doesn't follow our plans. Patience is a quiet strength that only grows during trials, adversities, and everyday frustrations—usually without us even realizing it.

The more we practice patience, the more we realize that it's not about being passive—it's about being strong enough to wait without giving up. This chapter will explore what it means to wait well, especially when we're trusting God for things that take time.

Patience means waiting calmly without getting angry, anxious, or upset when things don't happen as quickly as you want them to. It's the ability to trust that some things take time and that not everything *needs* to happen right away. Whether it's waiting in a long line, sitting through a delay, or hoping for something that hasn't come yet—patience is the quiet strength to stay calm and keep your peace.

Like other qualities in this book, patience is best learned through experience. Even though it is often learned the hard way, patience leaves us with something extremely valuable: a deeper trust in God's timing. As we develop this quiet strength, we begin to understand that waiting is not wasted time—it's preparation. Through patience, we become more grounded, more peaceful, and more open to the work God is doing in us while we wait.

Why Patience Matters

We live in a world where so much is instant. We can send a message in seconds, stream a movie right away, or get food delivered in minutes. But the most meaningful things in life—like strong relationships, spiritual growth, and character—can't be rushed. They take time.

Patience helps us slow down and trust the process. It teaches us to let go of the need for everything to happen in our timeline and reminds us to give others—and ourselves—more grace when things go differently than expected. It also helps us stay grounded in the truth that God is always working, even when we can't see the results right away.

Patience also strengthens our relationships. When we allow others the time and space to grow, make mistakes, and learn, we reflect the same mercy and understanding we hope to receive. It teaches us to listen more carefully, to be present in the moment, and to handle tension without letting emotions take over. Over time, patience helps build trust, compassion, and stronger bonds with the people around us.

"But if we hope for what we do not yet have, we wait for it patiently." – Romans 8:25

For Example...

Imagine you're excited about a prayer you've been praying for a long time—like for a friend, a dream, or a big opportunity. Day after day, it feels like nothing is changing. Patience helps you keep trusting that God hears you, even when the answer hasn't come yet.

Or maybe you're working on a goal—like improving your grades, learning a skill, or growing in a habit. Progress is slow, and you're tempted to give up. Patience reminds you that growth happens one step at a time, and each step is part of the journey.

This connects closely with what we've already learned in the chapters on perseverance and trust—because to be patient, you also need to be willing to keep going and believe that God's timing is always right.

Patience and Waiting on God

Some of the hardest moments in life are the ones when we're waiting for something that really matters. We want healing, answers, direction, or a breakthrough. And in those moments, it can feel like God is silent. This silence can be frustrating, disheartening, and even scary. But patience in faith means choosing to trust Him anyway.

Waiting on God also strengthens our trust. It teaches us to depend on His wisdom instead of our own and reminds us that His timing is always better than ours. Even when we don't get what we want right away—or at all—we can grow in patience by remembering that God sees the whole picture. Every season of waiting can become an opportunity to deepen our faith, if we're willing to let it.

> *"The Lord is good to those whose hope is in him, to the one who seeks him; it is good to wait quietly for the salvation of the Lord."* – Lamentations 3:25–26

Jesus Modeled Patience

When we think about patience, the best example we can look to is Jesus. He showed incredible patience throughout His life—waiting 30 years before beginning His public ministry, even though He was fully God the whole time. He patiently taught His disciples, even when they didn't understand or made mistakes.

Jesus always responded with compassion to people who doubted Him, rejected Him, or constantly asked for signs and miracles. And even when He was being mistreated, Jesus chose to stay calm and faithful to God's plan rather than fighting back or giving up.

Jesus' life reminds us that patience isn't weakness—it's strength under control. It's trusting that God's timing is perfect and choosing to love people even when they're difficult. If Jesus, the Son of God, was willing to wait and walk patiently with others, we can follow His example in our own lives. Whether you're waiting for something to change or learning to be patient with people around you, remember that patience makes you more like Christ.

Breakout Points

Quick Takeaway: Patience is trusting God's timing—
even when the waiting is hard.

Faith in Action: The next time you feel impatient, take
a deep breath and say a quick prayer: "God, help me
wait patiently."

Think About This: Why do you think God often uses waiting as a way to grow us?

Did You Know? The fruit of the Spirit in Galatians 5
includes patience as a sign of someone who is walking
closely with God.

❓ DISCUSSION QUESTIONS

1. What's something in your life right now that requires patience?

2. How do you usually respond when things don't happen as fast as you want them to?

3. Can you think of a time when waiting actually helped you grow?

4. Why do you think patience is important in your relationship with God?

5. How can you practice patience with people around you this week?

▶ ACTION CHALLENGE

Pick one situation this week where you know you'll need patience—maybe with a sibling, at school, or while waiting for something. When it happens, pause, take a breath, and ask God to help you respond with grace instead of frustration.

💬 FINAL THOUGHTS

Patience isn't just about waiting—it's about how we wait. It's about trusting God when things are quiet, slow, or unclear. And it's about treating others with the same grace we hope to receive when we're not at our best.

The next time you're tempted to rush ahead or lose your temper, remember: God is patient with us every single day.

We can learn to reflect that same patience in how we live, love, and trust Him.

🙏 CLOSING PRAYER

"Dear God, thank You for being so patient with me. Help me to grow in patience and to trust Your perfect timing. Teach me to wait well, to be kind when things don't go my way, and to believe that You're always working— even in the waiting. Amen."

CHAPTER 11

Humility

"Do nothing out of selfish ambition or vain conceit. Rather, in humility value others above yourselves, not looking to your own interests but each of you to the interests of the others."

– Philippians 2:3-4

Pride is often loud and attention-seeking, but humility is quiet confidence rooted in who God says you are. It doesn't need to prove itself or compete with others. In a world that often praises self-promotion and personal achievement, humility invites us to take a different path—one that puts God and others first.

Humility reminds us that strength isn't just found in boldness, but in gentleness, service, and the willingness to learn. Like many other virtues in this book, humility builds on the qualities that come before it—especially patience, self-discipline, and trust.

Humility means not thinking too highly of yourself and being willing to put others first. It's recognizing that you don't have all the answers, and that it's okay to learn, grow, and admit when you're wrong. Humility isn't about putting yourself down—it's about seeing yourself clearly and remembering that your value comes from God, not from how important you seem to others.

A humble person listens well, serves others without needing attention, and gives credit rather than taking it. Humility opens your heart to correction and helps you become someone who lifts others up instead of trying to stand above them.

Why Humility Matters

Humility also helps you recognize your need for God. When you stop trying to do everything on your own, you open the door to deeper dependence on Him. That kind of humility leads to spiritual maturity—it helps you lean on God's wisdom instead of your own understanding. It reminds you that your worth isn't earned by performance or praise but is already secure because of who you are in Christ.

Humility also means letting your actions speak louder than your words. You don't need to sing your own praises or make sure everyone knows what you've done. When you live with quiet confidence and do the right thing, others will notice—and often, they'll speak well of you without you having to say a word.

God values humility because it makes room for Him to work in your heart. When you're humble, you're teachable. And when you're teachable, you're ready to become the person God created you to be.

"He guides the humble in what is right and teaches them his way." – Psalm 25:9

For Example...

Imagine you're part of a team project, and you have a great idea—but someone else gets the credit. Humility means letting it go and being happy the project was a success, even if you weren't in the spotlight.

Or maybe a friend points out a mistake you made. Your first reaction might be to defend yourself, but humility helps you pause, listen, and admit where you were wrong. That doesn't make you weak—it makes you strong in character.

This connects with earlier chapters like integrity and obedience—because a humble person is honest with themselves and willing to take responsibility. Humility helps us grow by helping us let go of pride.

Humble vs. Humbled

Choosing humility isn't always easy, especially in a world that tells us to promote ourselves and fight for attention. But the Bible reminds us that it's far better to live with humility than to be humbled later. In Luke 14, Jesus tells a parable about being invited to a banquet. He says not to sit in the place of honor, in case someone more important shows up and you're asked to move.

Instead, sit in a lower place so the host can invite you to move up. *"For all those who exalt themselves will be humbled, and those who humble themselves will be exalted."* (Luke 14:11) This teaches us to let others—and God—lift us up rather than trying to lift ourselves.

In Matthew 20:16, Jesus also says, *"So the last will be first, and the first will be last."* This means that in God's kingdom, status and recognition don't matter the way they do in the world. What matters is the posture of your heart.

True humility isn't about being overlooked—it's about being willing to serve, to love, and to put others before yourself. And in the end, God honors those who quietly live with humility far more than those who try to take the spotlight for themselves.

Humility Like Jesus

Jesus is the perfect example of humility. He is the Son of God, yet He came to earth not to be served, but to serve. He washed His disciples' feet, spent time with people others looked down on, and gave His life for us. If anyone ever had the right to demand honor and praise, it was Jesus—but instead, He chose humility.

Jesus' humility was also deeply connected to His patience. He didn't rush to prove Himself or demand recognition, even when people doubted Him or misunderstood His mission. He patiently endured betrayal from one of His closest followers, which led to the humiliation and torture He experienced on the cross. Jesus showed that true humility trusts God's timing and willingly puts others' needs above personal comfort or glory.

When we follow His example, we begin to understand that true strength doesn't come from being better than others. It comes from being willing to love, serve, and forgive— even when no one notices.

> *"All of you, clothe yourselves with humility toward one another, because, 'God opposes the proud but shows favor to the humble.' Humble yourselves, therefore, under God's mighty hand, that he may lift you up in due time."*
>
> – 1 Peter 5:5-6

Breakout Points

Quick Takeaway: Humility is choosing to lift others up instead of trying to stand above them.

Faith in Action: Look for one opportunity this week to serve someone quietly, without needing to be noticed or thanked.

Think About This: Why do you think humility makes it easier to learn and grow?

Did You Know? The Bible says that *"God opposes the proud but gives grace to the humble."* (James 4:6)

❓ DISCUSSION QUESTIONS

1. What does humility mean to you?
2. Can you think of a time when you let someone else go first, speak first, or be in the spotlight?
3. Why is it hard to admit when we're wrong? How can humility help?
4. What does it look like to follow Jesus' example of humility?
5. How does humility strengthen your relationships with others?

▶ ACTION CHALLENGE

This week, find a way to put someone else first—maybe by helping quietly, listening without interrupting, or letting someone else have the credit. Practice humility by choosing to serve without needing recognition.

💬 FINAL THOUGHTS

Humility doesn't mean thinking less of yourself. It means thinking of yourself less and focusing more on others and on God. A humble heart is open to learning, full of gratitude, and willing to grow.

When you live with humility, people will notice—not because you're trying to be seen, but because you reflect the love and character of Jesus. And that kind of humility leaves a lasting impact.

🙏 CLOSING PRAYER

"Dear God, thank You for showing me what true humility looks like through Jesus. Help me to put others first, to listen well, and to serve with love. Teach me to be humble in my heart and confident in Your grace. Amen."

_____

CHAPTER 12

Gratitude

"Give thanks in all circumstances; for this is God's will for you in Christ Jesus."

– 1 Thessalonians 5:18

Gratitude is the natural outflow of a heart shaped by faith, trust, obedience, humility, patience, and the other virtues we've covered so far. It's the result of seeing life not through entitlement or comparison, but through appreciation. When we understand that everything we have is ultimately a gift from God, we begin to recognize how deeply we depend on Him.

Without the foundation of these other character qualities, gratitude often turns into pride or expectation. But with them, it becomes a wellspring of joy, contentment, and perspective. A grateful person is rarely conceited—because they know they've been given more than they deserve.

Gratitude is more than just saying "thank you." It's a mindset—a way of seeing life. It means choosing to notice and appreciate the blessings in your life, even when things aren't perfect. Gratitude is about focusing on what you have instead of what you've lost or the things you want.

When we live with gratitude, we recognize that every good thing we have is a gift from God. We stop taking things for granted—our family, our friends, our health, our daily needs—and we start seeing how much we truly have to be thankful for. Gratitude helps us stay grounded in joy, even in hard times.

Why Gratitude Matters

Gratitude changes our perspective. When we're thankful, we're less likely to complain, compare ourselves to others, or feel entitled. Gratitude reminds us that we aren't the center of the universe. It helps us become more patient, kind, and generous—because when you're thankful, you want to share that joy with others.

This chapter builds on what we learned in humility and patience. A humble heart recognizes that we don't earn everything on our own. A patient heart learns to wait without bitterness. Gratitude ties in to both, helping us trust that God knows what we need and will provide in His perfect timing.

Gratitude also fuels resilience and hope. When we practice gratitude, especially in difficult moments, we begin to see challenges as opportunities rather than obstacles. Instead of focusing on what's missing, we focus on how God is moving—even in ways we don't fully understand yet. This mindset doesn't erase hardship, but it gives us strength to persevere with a heart that remains soft and open, rather than hardened or bitter.

> "Do not be anxious about anything, but in every situation, by prayer and petition, with thanksgiving, present your requests to God." – Philippians 4:6

For Example...

Imagine someone gives you a gift—not because you earned it, but just because they care. How you respond matters. Do you toss it aside and ask for something better? Or do you say thank you and treat it with appreciation? Gratitude helps you see the value in what you've been given, whether it's a gift, a helping hand, or even a tough lesson.

The greatest gift we've ever been given is the sacrifice Jesus made for us on the cross. He gave His life so that we could be forgiven and have eternal life—and the only thing we have to do is accept that gift. Some people believe we have to earn our way into heaven by doing enough good things, but that would mean Jesus' death wasn't enough.

If someone gives you a gift, you don't have to work for it—it wouldn't be a gift if you did. Because of what Jesus has done, we should live our lives in a way that shows we're thankful—not to earn His love, but to honor it. Gratitude for His sacrifice should shape how we live, love, and treat others every day.

Obviously, gratitude is easiest when life is going well. But the real test of gratitude comes when things are hard. Can you still thank God when the answer to your prayer is "not yet"? Can you be thankful for what you have, even when it's not what you hoped for? That's when gratitude becomes an act of faith.

Gratitude in Action

Jesus often gave thanks, even in situations where others might have complained. Before feeding thousands with just a few loaves and fish, He gave thanks. Before facing the cross, He gave thanks. Gratitude wasn't just something Jesus felt when it was convenient—it was something He practiced constantly.

Just like Jesus demonstrated, practicing gratitude starts with a daily posture of the heart. Taking time each day to pause, pray, and thank God for His blessings—both big and small—helps shift our focus from what's missing to what's already been given.

Reflecting on answered prayers, recalling moments of joy, or simply being present and aware of God's goodness trains our minds to look for the positive, even in hard times. Practicing gratitude inwardly helps build a steady foundation of peace and contentment.

Finally, gratitude also grows stronger when we express it outwardly. Writing a note of thanks, encouraging a friend, or simply pausing to thank God out loud can deepen your awareness of His goodness. These outward acts don't just bless others—they reinforce your own thankfulness and shift your heart toward joy. When we turn our gratitude into action, it becomes more than a feeling—it becomes a habit that shapes how we live and how we love.

"Every good and perfect gift is from above, coming down from the Father of the heavenly lights." – James 1:17

Breakout Points

Quick Takeaway: Gratitude is choosing to focus on what you have, not what you lack.

Faith in Action: Start a "gratitude list." Write down three things you're thankful for every day this week.

Think About This: When was the last time you thanked God for something you normally take for granted?

Did You Know? Studies show that people who practice gratitude regularly are less stressed and more joyful. It's not just good for your heart—it's good for your mind, too.

❷ DISCUSSION QUESTIONS

1. What is something you've taken for granted that you want to start being more thankful for?

2. How does gratitude help you feel closer to God?

3. What's the difference between saying thank you and truly feeling thankful?

4. Can you think of a time when being thankful helped you feel better, even in a tough situation?

5. How can you show gratitude to others in your life?

⏵ ACTION CHALLENGE

Each day this week, thank someone for something they've done—even if it's something small. Write a note, say it out loud, or say a prayer thanking God for that person.

💬 FINAL THOUGHTS

Gratitude doesn't mean pretending everything is perfect. It means choosing to look for the good, even in the middle of challenges. It helps us focus on God's blessings and reminds us of His faithfulness, no matter what's happening around us.

Grateful people shine. They lift up others, reflect God's love, and make the world a better place—one thankful heart at a time.

✨ CLOSING PRAYER

"Dear God, thank You for all the blessings in my life—big and small. Help me to be thankful every day, not just when things go my way. Teach me to see Your goodness, even when life is hard. Fill my heart with gratitude and help me share that joy with others. Amen."

CHAPTER 13

Grace

> "For it is by grace you have been saved, through faith—and this is not from yourselves, it is the gift of God—not by works, so that no one can boast."
>
> – Ephesians 2:8-9

This chapter marks a shift in focus—from character traits that strengthen us inwardly, to those that also bless and build up the people around us. Please don't misunderstand— qualities like faith, integrity, patience, and humility absolutely have an outward impact. When you live them out, others will notice. Your example can inspire change in those around you, encouraging them to adopt these values in their own lives.

But the character traits in the chapters ahead—starting with grace—are especially powerful because they are designed to flow outward first. They are actions we intentionally take to serve, encourage, and uplift others. And yet, the beauty of these outward expressions is that they still work within us, too—softening our hearts, strengthening our relationships, and drawing us closer to God in the process.

The last chapter on gratitude closed by exploring how a thankful heart expresses appreciation both inwardly and outwardly. Grace is the natural partner to that kind of heart. Gratitude helps us recognize what we've received, and grace moves us to extend kindness and forgiveness to others, as well as ourselves. Grace is what allows us to let go of bitterness, shame, or hurt that might otherwise harden our hearts.

Grace means giving kindness, forgiveness, or favor even when the person/people don't deserve it or haven't earned it. When someone gives you grace, it's like getting a second chance when you didn't think it would ever happen. Grace is at the very heart of how God treats us—loving us even when we mess up—and giving us good things we could never earn on our own.

God's grace isn't based on what we do or how good we are. It's freely given, without conditions. Because we receive grace freely from God, He also calls us to show grace to others. Grace helps us forgive, be patient, and give second chances—because we know we need those things, too.

Why Grace Matters

Grace matters because it changes everything. Without grace, our mistakes would define us and we'd carry around guilt and shame every day. Thankfully, grace frees us from that weight. It lets us start fresh, knowing God's love is stronger than our biggest failures.

Without the ability to move forward, we stay stuck—whether it's stuck in our own guilt or in resentment toward someone else. Grace gives us a way to release what we can't change and trust God with what comes next. It doesn't ignore the wrongs that have been done, but it makes room for healing, growth, and restored relationships. Living in grace means making peace with the past so you can step into the future with hope.

This chapter builds on previous chapters like humility, gratitude, and patience. To show grace, you need humility—to recognize you're not perfect, either. You also need gratitude—to remember how much grace you've already received. Grace helps us become more patient and understanding because we know we're all growing and learning together.

> *"But he said to me, 'My grace is sufficient for you, for my power is made perfect in weakness.'"*
>
> – 2 Corinthians 12:9

For Example...

Imagine accidentally breaking something important to your family. Instead of getting angry, your parents say, *"It's okay. We know you didn't mean it."* That's grace. They have every right to be upset, but they choose forgiveness instead.

Or think about a friend who hurts your feelings. You could choose to stay angry or hold a grudge—but grace means forgiving them, even though they might not deserve it. Grace doesn't excuse what happened, but it gives the relationship a chance to heal and grow stronger.

What about if you make a mistake and ruin something you've spent a lot of time on? Sometimes the hardest person to give grace to is yourself. We often hold on to mistakes we've made and replay them in our minds. Grace helps us let go, forgive ourselves, and remember God sees us with compassion and love, not disappointment.

Receiving Grace Without Shame

In that same breath, sometimes the hardest part about grace isn't giving it to others—it's receiving it ourselves. Many people carry a deep sense of shame or unworthiness, believing they've messed up too badly or fallen too far for God to forgive them. They might know in their minds that grace is a gift, but their hearts struggle to accept it. This can lead to harsh self-judgment, lingering guilt, or even a fear of getting close to God.

But grace was never about being worthy—it's about God's love being bigger than our flaws. The Bible reminds us that while we were still sinners, Christ died for us. That means grace comes before we ever "get it all together." It's not a reward for the good—it's a gift for the broken. Learning to receive that kind of love can be hard, but it opens the door to real healing and freedom.

If you ever see someone else struggling with shame or self-doubt, don't look away. Come alongside them. Offer encouragement, kindness, and truth. Remind them they're not alone and that no mistake is too great for God's mercy. Grace isn't just something we receive—it's something we pass along to others who might not believe they deserve it. That's when grace becomes real and powerful.

> *"And let us consider how we may spur one another on toward love and good deeds, not giving up meeting together... but encouraging one another..."*
>
> – 2 Corinthians 12:9

Grace Given Freely

The greatest example of grace is Jesus. He willingly gave His life to pay for our sins—not because we earned it, but because He loves us deeply. Jesus showed grace to people who were rejected by others, like the woman at the well, the dishonest tax collector, or Zacchaeus. He didn't wait for them to earn forgiveness. He gave it freely.

Grace reminds us that our relationship with God isn't about trying harder or doing more to impress Him. It's about accepting what He's already done for us. When we truly understand grace, it transforms the way we see ourselves, others, and God.

"Be kind and compassionate to one another, forgiving each other, just as in Christ God forgave you."

– Ephesians 4:32

Breakout Points

Quick Takeaway: Grace means giving and receiving kindness and forgiveness, even when it's undeserved.

Faith in Action: This week, choose one person in your life to show grace to—someone who's upset you or made a mistake. Pray for them and find a way to show kindness instead of anger.

Think About This: Can you remember a time when someone showed you grace? How did it feel?

Did You Know? Mercy means not giving someone what they deserve—like punishment. Grace means giving someone what they don't deserve—like forgiveness.

❷ DISCUSSION QUESTIONS

1. Why do you think grace is so powerful?

2. How does it feel when someone gives you grace after you've made a mistake?

3. Why can it be so difficult to show grace to others sometimes?

4. Why is it important to remember God's grace when we think about our own mistakes?

5. How can practicing grace make your relationships stronger?

⏵ ACTION CHALLENGE

This week, write down something you're holding onto—maybe a mistake you made, or something someone did to hurt you. Pray about it, ask God for the strength to show grace, and then let it go.

💬 FINAL THOUGHTS

Grace doesn't mean pretending mistakes never happened—it means choosing forgiveness and love instead of anger or bitterness. When you practice grace, you reflect the very heart of Jesus, who gave everything so we could know forgiveness and freedom.

Live each day in grace, knowing God loves you deeply. Allow yourself and others the freedom to make mistakes and grow. Grace brings healing, hope, and strength.

🙏 CLOSING PRAYER

"Dear God, thank You for Your amazing grace. Help me remember how much You love me, even when I mess up. Teach me to show grace to others, forgiving them just as You forgive me. Fill my heart with Your grace and help me live each day grateful for Your unconditional love. Amen."

CHAPTER 14

Respect

"Do to others as you would have them do to you."

– Luke 6:31

Respect is one of the most outward-facing character traits we can practice—but it also shapes us inwardly. When we honor others, we show them they matter to us and to God. And as we treat people with care, dignity, and understanding, it reminds us of our own worth, too.

Respect invites connection and builds bridges, and it becomes even more meaningful when it grows from a heart shaped by faith, humility, and grace. When we've developed the inward strength and values from previous chapters, showing respect isn't just a reaction—it becomes who we are.

Respect means treating people with kindness, honor, and value. It's how we show others that they matter—not just because of what they do, but because of who they are. Respect is shown through our words, our tone, our actions, and even our body language. It means listening when someone is talking, being polite even when we disagree, and showing care for people's feelings and boundaries.

Respect isn't just something we give to people who are older than us or those in authority—it's something we give to everyone, because every person is made in the image of God. Whether it's a friend, a teacher, a parent, a coworker, a classmate, or someone we don't even know, respect reminds us to treat others the way we want to be treated.

Respect Starts with You

As important as it is to respect others, you need to first have self-respect. Self-respect is knowing that your life has value because God made you and loves you. It means understanding that you are not defined by your mistakes, your appearance, or what other people say about you.

When you have self-respect, you speak kindly to yourself. You appreciate yourself and give yourself grace. You take care of your mind, body, and spirit, and you set boundaries that protect your heart. People who respect themselves are more likely to respect others—and they're also more likely to walk away from situations or relationships that are harmful or unhealthy.

Please don't ever forget that you *deserve* to be respected. If you are in any type of relationship where the other person or people continually disrespect you, gracefully remove them from your life. Setting boundaries isn't mean—it's wise, and it's one of the clearest ways to show that you value the person God made you to be.

"*I praise you because I am fearfully and wonderfully made; your works are wonderful, I know that full well.*"

– Psalm 139:14

Why Respect Matters

Respect helps build trust, peace, and understanding in our relationships. When we treat people with respect, we invite them to do the same. Even when we don't see eye to eye with someone, showing respect communicates that we value them as a person.

Respect also reflects our relationship with God. When we show respect to others, we honor the fact that they are His creation. And when we carry ourselves with self-respect, we're saying, *"I believe God made me for a purpose, and I'm going to live like that's true."*

Additionally, respect helps us navigate difficult moments with wisdom and maturity. It reminds us that we can stand firm in our beliefs without tearing others down. When we respond to conflict with a respectful attitude, we not only protect our own peace, but we often de-escalate tension and open the door to healthier conversations. In a world where disrespect is often loud and constant, choosing respect sets you apart as someone others can trust and admire.

"Be devoted to one another in love. Honor one another above yourselves." – Romans 12:10

For Example...

Think about how you feel when someone talks over you, rolls their eyes, or makes fun of you in front of others. It doesn't feel good—and that's why respect matters. Now think about how it feels when someone listens carefully, responds kindly, and treats you with care. That's what respect looks like in action.

Let's say a friend gets on your nerves and you're tempted to snap back. Respect means pausing, taking a breath, and choosing words that are kind and thoughtful.

Or maybe you make a mistake and start calling yourself names in your head. Self-respect means stopping that negative talk and reminding yourself, *"I messed up, but I'm still loved, and I can do better next time."*

Respect Is a Choice

Sometimes it's easy to show respect—like when you're with someone you admire or agree with. But real respect is tested when you're frustrated, misunderstood, or around someone who treats you poorly. It takes strength to stay calm, speak with kindness, and set boundaries without being mean.

Respect doesn't mean you let people walk all over you. It means you can disagree without being disrespectful, and you can walk away from unkindness without returning it. It's not a sign of weakness—it's a sign of strength and character.

When you have self-respect, you understand your worth and set healthy boundaries. You're less likely to stay in situations or relationships that make you feel small or devalued. People who struggle with self-respect may allow mistreatment because they feel they don't deserve better— or they may make choices that lead to pain because they believe they're not worthy of a better outcome. But God doesn't see you that way, and you shouldn't either.

Choosing to respect yourself means speaking to yourself with kindness, expecting to be treated with care, and believing that you are worth protecting and standing up for. When you know your value—and more importantly, how much God values you—you'll be more confident in treating others with the same level of respect and grace.

"So in everything, do to others what you would have them do to you, for this sums up the Law and the Prophets."

– Matthew 7:12

Breakout Points

Quick Takeaway: Respect is treating others—and yourself—with kindness, value, and care.

Faith in Action: Find one way today to show respect to someone who might not expect it. A kind word, a patient response, or even just listening can go a long way.

Think About This: Do you speak to yourself with the same kindness you show to others?

Did You Know? You can disagree with someone and still treat them with respect. It's not about always agreeing—it's about always being kind.

❓ DISCUSSION QUESTIONS

1. How do you feel when someone shows you respect? How about when they don't?

2. Why is it important to show respect to everyone—not just people in authority?

3. What does self-respect look like in your everyday life?

4. Have you ever had to choose respect, even when it was difficult?

5. What are some ways you can grow in how you respect others and yourself?

▶ ACTION CHALLENGE

Pick one person in your life who you sometimes find difficult to respect. Make it your goal this week to show them respect through your actions or words. Also, write down three things you like about yourself to remind you of your own value.

💬 FINAL THOUGHTS

Respect and self-respect go hand in hand. When you treat others with kindness and show yourself that same grace, you build stronger relationships and a healthier view of yourself. God made each of us with value—and when we live like that's true, we become people who lift others up instead of tearing them down.

Respect isn't just about being nice. It's about recognizing the worth in every person, including yourself, and choosing to act in a way that honors that worth...every single day!

⛰ CLOSING PRAYER

"Dear God, help me to show respect in all I say and do. Remind me that every person is made in Your image— including me. Teach me to speak kindly, to listen well, and to treat others and myself with honor and care. Thank You for creating me with value and purpose. Amen."

CHAPTER 15

Generosity

"Each of you should give what you have decided
in your heart to give, not reluctantly or under
compulsion, for God loves a cheerful giver."

– 2 Corinthians 9:7

This chapter continues our focus on the outward expressions of a strong, God-centered character. While previous qualities like faith, patience, and humility shape us from the inside out, generosity is a clear way we demonstrate what's been built within. It's a response to all the grace, forgiveness, and blessings we've received—and a reflection of how deeply we've come to understand what it means to live a life shaped by God's love.

True generosity flows from a grateful heart and becomes one of the most powerful ways to bless others, build connection, and point people toward Him. Jesus Himself compels us to be generous by serving others—He set the ultimate example in Mark 10:45, saying, *"For even the Son of Man did not come to be served, but to serve, and to give his life as a ransom for many."* When we follow His lead, our generosity becomes more than kindness—it becomes a reflection of His love.

Generosity is choosing to give freely from your heart, whether it's your time, money, talents, or simply kindness. It means focusing more on how you can help others than on what you can keep for yourself. Generosity isn't just about what you have or how much you give—it's about why you give and the spirit behind your actions.

Generous people see their blessings not as things to hold tightly, but as opportunities to share. Generosity isn't just giving away extra; it's willingly sharing even when you don't have much. It's about having an open heart, trusting God, and wanting others to feel loved and cared for.

Why Generosity Matters

Generosity matters because it changes lives—both yours and the lives of those around you. When you're generous, you reflect God's love, which is the greatest generosity of all. Everything we have ultimately comes from God and generosity reminds us that we are stewards, not owners, of what we've been given.

When you give generously, you build stronger relationships and communities. People trust you more because they see you care genuinely about their well-being. Generosity also brings joy—not just to the person receiving, but to you as well. Giving truly is more rewarding than receiving.

Generosity also shifts our mindset from scarcity to abundance. When we live with open hands instead of closed fists, we begin to notice just how much we have to give— encouragement, compassion, time, wisdom, or kindness. And as we practice generosity, our confidence in God's provision grows stronger.

It helps us stop worrying so much about what we might lose and start noticing how much we can give. Generosity becomes not just an action, but a way of living that honors God and brings light into the lives of others.

> *"And God is able to bless you abundantly, so that in all things at all times, having all that you need, you will abound in every good work."* – 2 Corinthians 9:8

For Example...

Imagine your family has leftovers after dinner. Generosity might look like giving some to a neighbor who's sick or going through a hard time. Or maybe you have a friend who forgot their lunch at school—generosity means sharing yours without expecting anything back.

Generosity doesn't always involve giving physical things. It can also mean giving your time to someone who needs it, like helping a classmate with homework, listening patiently to a friend who's having a tough day, or volunteering your skills to make someone's life easier.

Generosity means being willing to go out of your way to make a difference in the lives of others. And while giving generously often blesses others greatly, you might find that you are the one most blessed in the end.

Generosity and the Heart

Most people think of generosity as simply giving money or things, but true generosity is deeper than that and it begins in your heart. It's about having an attitude of kindness and compassion that looks for ways to serve. Sometimes generosity means forgiving someone who hurt you or offering friendship to someone who feels left out.

Remember the widow's offering in the Bible (Mark 12:41-44). Jesus saw people giving large sums of money, but He praised a poor widow who gave just two small coins—everything she had. Generosity isn't measured by the amount given, but by the heart behind it. God values the sincerity, sacrifice, and love that motivate our gifts.

> *"Give generously to them and do so without a grudging heart; then because of this the Lord your God will bless you in all your work and in everything you put your hand to."* – Matthew 6:3-4

Giving in Secret

Generosity isn't about getting attention or impressing others—it's about quietly honoring God by meeting the needs of people around us. In fact, the Bible encourages us to give in secret. Jesus said, *"But when you give to the needy, do not let your left hand know what your right hand is doing, so that your giving may be in secret. Then your Father, who sees what is done in secret, will reward you."* – Deuteronomy 15:10

This kind of giving protects our hearts from pride. It reminds us that we don't give to be noticed—we give because it's the right thing to do and because God sees every act of kindness, no matter how small. True generosity comes from a place of humility. It doesn't need applause or approval because it already knows God is pleased.

God loves a cheerful giver—not one who gives reluctantly or out of pressure, but someone who gives freely, from the heart. When we give quietly and joyfully, we're placing our trust in God to reward us in His own perfect way. And His rewards are far greater than anything we could gain from human recognition.

> *"Be careful not to practice your righteousness in front of others to be seen by them. If you do, you will have no reward from your Father in heaven."* – Matthew 6:1

Breakout Points

Quick Takeaway: Generosity is giving freely and cheerfully from the heart, no matter how big or small the gift.

Faith in Action: Find one specific way this week to give generously—whether it's donating clothes you no longer need, spending time helping someone, or just being extra kind to those around you.

Think About This: When was a time someone was generous with you? How did that impact your day or your feelings toward them?

Did You Know? Studies show generous people tend to be happier, less stressed, and feel more connected to others.

❷ DISCUSSION QUESTIONS

1. Why do you think God loves a cheerful giver?

2. How can you practice generosity even if you don't have money or physical things to give away?

3. What's the difference between giving generously and giving reluctantly?

4. Can you think of someone who has shown great generosity? What did you learn from their example?

5. How do you feel when you give generously to others?

⏵ ACTION CHALLENGE

This week, set aside some time or resources to help someone in need. Do it joyfully, without expecting recognition or reward. **Bonus challenge:** Do something generous for someone this week without letting anyone know it was you. Afterward, take a moment to thank God for the opportunity to be a blessing.

💬 FINAL THOUGHTS

Generosity isn't about giving away everything you own or having all the answers. It's simply opening your heart to share what you have by remembering how generously God has blessed you. When you choose generosity, you become more like Jesus, who gave everything for us.

God has promised that when you're generous, you'll never lack what you need. In fact, generosity often brings unexpected blessings back to you, creating a cycle of kindness that continues to grow.

🙏 CLOSING PRAYER

"Dear God, thank You for generously blessing me in so many ways. Teach me to be generous, too, to share freely, and to give cheerfully. Let me reflect Your kindness and love to others every day. Amen."

CHAPTER 16

Confidence

"So do not throw away your confidence; it will
be richly rewarded. You need to persevere so
that when you have done the will of God, you will
receive what he has promised."

– Hebrews 10:35–36

Confidence may be one of the most misunderstood character traits—often mistaken for arrogance or selfishness. But true confidence is something much deeper. It comes from an inner assurance that you are deeply known and loved by God. Like the previous chapters have shown, when we have qualities like humility, grace, and patience, they help create a steady foundation for healthy, God-centered confidence.

Confidence built on faith is both inwardly strengthening and outwardly inspiring—it helps us walk in boldness without needing to prove ourselves. And when it's rooted in God, it becomes a source of peace, courage, and quiet strength. It's believing that God made you for a purpose and trusting that He has given you everything you need to live with courage, strength, and meaning. True confidence is rooted in knowing who you are *in Christ*.

Confidence helps you step into situations—even scary ones—with faith that God is with you. It allows you to try new things, speak up when something needs to be said, and face challenges without fear of failure. So even if you do fail, you can move forward knowing that failure is not the end of the road.

Every mistake is a chance to learn, grow, and become stronger in both your character and your faith. Confidence doesn't mean you'll never feel nervous or unsure—it just means you know where your strength comes from.

Confidence vs. Pride

It's important to know that confidence is not the same as pride. Pride says, *"I can do this on my own."* Confidence says, *"I can do this because God is with me."* Pride puts the spotlight on yourself. Confidence puts the spotlight on the God who created you, loves you, and equips you.

When your confidence is rooted in God, it doesn't go up and down depending on how successful, popular, or talented you feel. It stays steady because you know your worth doesn't come from people—it comes from your Creator.

> *"It is better to take refuge in the Lord than to trust in humans."* – Psalm 118:8

Why Confidence Matters

When you have confidence, you're more willing to take healthy risks, stand up for what's right, and use your gifts to serve others. You stop comparing yourself to everyone around you and start focusing on becoming better than the person you were yesterday.

Confidence helps you grow. It helps you learn from your mistakes instead of being crushed by them. It gives you the boldness to say, *"I'm not perfect, but I'm willing to keep trying."* And most importantly, confidence allows you to live in freedom—not trying to impress people, but living to please God. When your confidence comes from Him, you don't have to be afraid of falling short—you just keep moving forward, trusting that He's shaping you through the process.

That's because confidence doesn't disappear just because you fail—it actually gets stronger when you keep going in spite of setbacks. No one starts out perfect. Whether you're learning something new, stepping into leadership, or growing in your faith, there will be moments when things don't go the way you hoped. That's okay. Failure isn't the opposite of growth—it's part of it. Each time you mess up and try again, you're building wisdom, strength, and the kind of courage that leads to lasting confidence.

> *"Not only so, but we also glory in our sufferings, because we know that suffering produces perseverance; perseverance, character; and character, hope."*

> – Romans 5:3-4

Confidence also empowers others. When you live with quiet confidence—without needing to be the loudest or the most noticed—you create space for others to shine, too. Your example can help others believe in themselves and trust in God's work in their lives. And when you lift others up with your words or actions, it doesn't take anything away from you—instead, it multiplies the strength and courage in the people around you.

For Example...

Think about someone who decides to introduce them-selves to a new group or speak up when they normally stay quiet. Or someone who's willing to try out for a team, sing in front of others, or invite a new student to sit with them. That's confidence in action—not because they know everything will go perfectly, but because they're willing to try anyway.

Confidence also shows up in quiet ways. It's in the person who apologizes first after an argument, or someone who stays true to their values even when it's unpopular. Confidence isn't loud or boastful—it's steady, humble, and faithful.

Confidence Grows Through Faith

Confidence doesn't grow by trying to be perfect. It grows by spending time with God, learning who He says you are, and trusting His promises. The more you understand that God is for you, the more confident you'll become—not in yourself, but in the One who made you.

Confidence also grows when you keep going, even after you fall. Every time you get back up and keep moving forward, you're building inner strength. Don't be afraid to fail. Be afraid of never trying because you didn't believe God could use you.

One more important part of confidence is trusting in God even when things don't go the way we hoped. Sometimes we pray for something and feel disappointed when the answer is "no" or "not yet." But God sees the bigger picture. Confidence means believing that He is still good, still present, and still working for our good—even when we don't get the outcome we wanted. Real confidence says, "I trust You, God; no matter what."

> *"Being confident of this, that he who began a good work in you will carry it on to completion until the day of Christ Jesus."* – Philippians 1:6

Breakout Points

Quick Takeaway: Confidence is believing in who God made you to be and trusting that He's with you in every step.

Faith in Action: When you feel unsure this week, remind yourself of a truth from Scripture that speaks to your identity in Christ.

Think About This: Are you placing your confidence in your abilities—or in God's power working through you?

Did You Know? The Bible is full of people who didn't feel confident at first—like Moses, Esther, and Jeremiah—but God used them in powerful ways because they trusted Him.

❓ DISCUSSION QUESTIONS

1. What's the difference between confidence and pride?
2. When have you felt confident in a way that honored God?
3. Why do you think God wants us to live with confidence?
4. What is one area of your life where you'd like to grow in confidence?
5. How can you encourage someone else to be confident in who God made them to be?

▶ ACTION CHALLENGE

Write down three specific areas in your life where you'd like to grow in confidence. Ask God to help you grow in these areas with humility, courage, and trust in His timing. Keep your list somewhere you can revisit as you take small steps forward.

💬 FINAL THOUGHTS

Confidence isn't about being the best or getting everything right. It's about knowing that you are loved, chosen, and equipped by God to do good things. You don't have to wait until you feel ready—God is ready to work in you and through you right now.

The more you trust Him, the more confident you'll become. And the more confident you are in Him, the more you'll be able to face life with courage, hope, and joy.

⚑ CLOSING PRAYER

"Dear God, thank You for creating me with purpose and value. Help me to put my confidence in You, not in what others think. Teach me to see myself through Your eyes and to trust Your plan for my life. Give me boldness to live for You every day. Amen."

CHAPTER 17

Accountability

"So then, each of us will give an account of ourselves to God."

– Romans 14:12

At this point in the journey, you've explored what it means to live with conviction, courage, integrity, self-discipline, humility, and more. Each of these character qualities is powerful on its own, but they only become lasting habits when we hold ourselves accountable to them. In many ways, accountability is the thread that ties them all together— it's the trait that makes every other one stick.

Accountability is what keeps you anchored. It's the follow-through that turns good intentions into real growth. Without it, even the strongest values can fade when life gets busy or tough. This chapter will show how accountability isn't just about owning your mistakes—it's about consistently living out everything you've learned and becoming someone others can rely on, and also someone God can work through.

Accountability means taking responsibility for your actions, choices, and behavior. It's being honest with yourself, with others, and with God. When you're accountable, you own your mistakes, admit when you've done something wrong, and take steps to make it right.

Being accountable doesn't mean you're expected to be perfect. It means you're willing to face the truth, learn from it, and grow. Accountability builds trust, strengthens relationships, and helps you become the kind of person others can count on—and the kind of person God calls you to be.

Why Accountability Matters

Accountability is what turns good intentions into real growth. It's easy to say you'll do something, but following through and being held to that promise takes maturity and character. When you take responsibility for your actions, you show that your words mean something.

It also creates space for learning. When you can admit a mistake, you give yourself a chance to grow from it. When you try to hide your mistakes or blame others, it keeps you stuck. But when you're honest, God can use your humility to shape you.

Accountability doesn't stop at admitting when you're wrong—it also means actively taking ownership of your commitments and responsibilities. When you're accountable, you understand your choices affect others, and you're willing to openly acknowledge when you've fallen short of what you've promised.

Rather than ignoring a commitment or making excuses, an accountable person communicates honestly and transparently, taking responsibility and making efforts to set things right. This honesty builds trust and strengthens relationships, showing others that even if things don't go perfectly, you're someone who faces challenges with integrity.

"Whoever conceals their sins does not prosper, but the one who confesses and renounces them finds mercy."

– Proverbs 28:13

For Example...

Imagine you said something hurtful in a moment of frustration. Accountability means going back and saying, *"That wasn't right. I'm sorry for what I said."* It's not always easy, but it shows that you value your relationships and are willing to grow.

Or maybe you promised your parents or a friend you'd help with something important, but you realize you're not going to be able to keep that promise. Instead of avoiding the issue or hoping they'll forget, accountability means openly acknowledging it. You could say, *"I know I promised I'd help, but I underestimated my schedule and now I won't be able to. I'm really sorry. Can we figure out another way I can help?"* Handling the situation honestly demonstrates that you care about your commitments and respect the people affected by your choices.

Accountability Means Being Open and Honest

Accountability isn't easy. It requires courage to face the truth, humility to admit when we've made mistakes, and maturity to take responsibility. Often, our first reaction when we mess up is to hide or make excuses. But hiding from our mistakes doesn't make them disappear—it only makes things worse. Instead, accountability invites us to honestly acknowledge what we've done and commit to doing better.

Part of accountability is repentance, which goes deeper than simply feeling sorry or regretful. True repentance is about openly acknowledging your mistake to God and to those you've wronged, and then actively making changes. The Bible says, *"If we confess our sins, he is faithful and just and will forgive us our sins and purify us from all unrighteousness"* (1 John 1:9).

God's grace is always there when we're willing to come to Him honestly and humbly. Repentance shows maturity, demonstrates humility, and reflects genuine accountability. The best part about repenting is that it brings us back into fellowship with God, allowing us to better experience His blessings.

Another essential aspect of accountability is allowing trusted people to speak into your life. Whether it's a parent, teacher, mentor, or close friend, it is vital to have someone who can help keep you accountable by gently and honestly pointing out your blind spots. This is also known as *constructive criticism.*

Receiving feedback isn't always comfortable and our first instinct might be defensiveness. However, being truly accountable means resisting that impulse. It means listening, reflecting, and making positive changes based on wise advice.

When you embrace accountability, you open yourself to growth and deeper relationships. You'll become someone others trust and rely upon, knowing that your actions match your words. Ultimately, accountability leads to a life that honors God, builds strong relationships, and shapes you into the person He has called you to be.

"Listen to advice and accept discipline, and at the end you will be counted among the wise." – Proverbs 19:20

Breakout Points

Quick Takeaway: Accountability is about owning your actions and being willing to grow from your mistakes.

Faith in Action: If you've made a mistake recently, take time to admit it, ask for forgiveness, and make it right.

Think About This: Who do you allow to speak truth into your life, even when it's uncomfortable?

Did You Know? The word "accountability" comes from the word "account," which means to explain or give a report of something. When we are accountable, we give a truthful report of our actions.

❷ DISCUSSION QUESTIONS

1. Why do you think it's sometimes hard to take responsibility for our mistakes?

2. Can you think of a time when you owned up to something, and it helped restore trust?

3. What can happen when people avoid accountability?

4. How can being accountable help you grow in your faith?

5. Who is someone in your life that helps keep you accountable in a loving way?

⏵ ACTION CHALLENGE

Think of one situation this week where you can practice accountability. Whether it's following through on a promise, admitting a mistake, or simply being honest about how you're doing—take responsibility and be real about it.

💬 FINAL THOUGHTS

Accountability may feel uncomfortable in the moment, but it leads to freedom, growth, and stronger relationships. It takes courage to admit when we're wrong, but every time we do, we become more trustworthy, more humble, and more like the person God is shaping us to be.

God doesn't expect perfection—He wants honesty. And when we're honest, He meets us with grace and gives us the strength to do better next time.

🙏 CLOSING PRAYER

"Dear God, help me to be honest about my actions and choices. Give me the humility to admit when I'm wrong and the courage to grow from my mistakes. Surround me with people who will speak truth into my life and help me stay on the right path. Thank You for Your grace and for never giving up on me. Amen."

___

CHAPTER 18

Leadership

"Instead, whoever wants to become great among you must be your servant, and whoever wants to be first must be your slave—just as the Son of Man did not come to be served, but to serve."

– Matthew 20:26-28

Good character brings opportunities to lead others. When you consistently live out the values we've explored throughout this book—like humility, integrity, courage, and respect—you naturally become someone others want to follow. Leadership isn't reserved for those with a title or a loud voice.

Some of the most impactful leaders are the ones who simply lead by example. Whether you realize it or not, your words, actions, and choices influence the people around you. And when you choose to live in a way that honors God, you become a leader in the best and truest sense.

Leadership isn't just about being in charge, giving orders, or getting attention. True leadership means guiding others by serving, inspiring, and helping them become the best they can be. Great leaders don't focus on making themselves look good; they focus on lifting up those around them.

The best kind of leadership is servant leadership—the kind Jesus modeled for us. He put others first, cared deeply about their needs, and used His influence to serve rather than to dominate. A leader worth following listens well, is humble enough to learn from others, and compassionate enough to care about the people they're leading.

Why Leadership Matters

Good leadership can change lives. Whether you realize it or not, someone is always watching you—siblings, friends, teammates, even adults. Your actions can inspire others to be better, kinder, stronger people. Leaders set the tone and shape the culture, and a good leader leaves things better than they found them.

This can be a big responsibility. When others begin to look up to you, your words and actions carry weight. That's why it's so important for leaders to stay grounded in character and faith. You won't always make perfect choices, but being a trustworthy leader means being honest, accountable, and committed to doing better. A faithful leader leads not just with their voice—but with their example. And when that example reflects the heart of Jesus, it inspires real and lasting change.

Jesus showed us the power of servant leadership when He washed His disciples' feet—a job usually reserved for servants. By humbly serving others, He demonstrated that real strength comes from humility, kindness, and sacrifice.

Leadership means recognizing your influence—big or small—and using it for good. It means looking for opportunities to serve rather than opportunities to be served.

God calls each of us to lead by example, reflecting the love, strength, and kindness of Jesus.

> "Now that I, your Lord and Teacher, have washed your feet, you also should wash one another's feet. I have set you an example that you should do as I have done for you." – John 13:14-15

For Example...

Imagine you're part of a team and one teammate is struggling. A good leader doesn't point out mistakes publicly or make the person feel bad. Instead, they privately encourage, help, and support that teammate so everyone succeeds together. Leadership is about building others up, not tearing them down.

Another example might be standing up for someone who's being treated unfairly. Even if you're nervous or afraid, choosing to speak up and do what's right is leadership in action. Your courage might inspire others to stand up, too.

Leadership Doesn't Have to Be Loud

It's easy to think that leadership only applies to those in charge of big groups or standing on a stage, but that's not true. You don't need to lead a crowd to be a leader. Sometimes, leadership means being a steady example for just one person—whether it's a younger sibling, a classmate, or a friend who's struggling. The influence you have on one life can be just as powerful as leading many.

Leadership can also be quiet. It doesn't always show up as bold speeches or public actions. Sometimes it looks like showing up consistently, choosing what's right when no one else does, or encouraging someone behind the scenes. Quiet leadership has the power to build trust, model humility, and inspire courage in others—without ever demanding attention.

Whether your influence feels big or small, it matters. God often uses those who lead quietly and faithfully to make the biggest difference. So don't wait to be chosen or noticed—lead right where you are, with kindness, integrity, and grace.

Leadership Starts Now

You don't need a title or position to be a leader. Leadership is about your choices, your character, and how you treat others each day. Whether it's helping at home, standing up to a bully at school, or simply being kind to someone who feels alone; leadership is found in your actions right now.

Being in a position of leadership often reveals your true character. Some people, when given authority, choose to use it selfishly—abusing their power simply because they can. These leaders let power go to their heads, thinking more about their own importance than the good of others.

This approach never leads to lasting success or respect. True leaders understand that leadership is not about having power—it's about using it wisely, humbly, and compassionately. The strongest leaders don't seek authority to serve themselves; they seek opportunities to serve and uplift others.

Finally, leadership also requires courage. Sometimes, you have to make decisions that aren't easy or popular, but you do them because they're right. Leaders stand up for others, speak out against unfairness, and hold themselves accountable.

"Don't let anyone look down on you because you are young, but set an example for the believers in speech, in conduct, in love, in faith and in purity."

– 1 Timothy 4:12

Breakout Points

Quick Takeaway: True leadership means serving and guiding others, not just being in charge.

Faith in Action: Look for ways you can serve others this week without expecting praise. Offer help at home, school, or church—quietly and joyfully.

Think About This: Who is someone you admire as a leader? What qualities make them worth following?

Did You Know? Many great leaders in the Bible—like Moses, David, Esther, and Paul—were humble and even uncertain at first. God uses *ordinary* people to do *extraordinary* things!

❓ DISCUSSION QUESTIONS

1. Why do you think servant leadership is so powerful?

2. Can you think of someone in your life who is a good example of leadership? What makes them a great leader?

3. How can you be a good leader even if you're not in a position of authority?

4. Why does leadership require humility and courage?

5. How does following Jesus' example change the way we lead others?

▶ ACTION CHALLENGE

This week, choose one specific way you can practice leadership by serving others—maybe helping a younger sibling, volunteering for a task at home or school, or simply being encouraging to someone who needs it.

💬 FINAL THOUGHTS

Leadership doesn't mean having all the answers or being perfect—it means having a heart that genuinely cares. A good leader helps others succeed, encourages them, and lives by example. When you lead like Jesus, with humility, courage, and compassion, you can truly change the world around you for the better.

🙏 CLOSING PRAYER

"Dear God, help me to be a leader who serves others just like Jesus did. Show me how to lead with kindness, courage, and humility. Give me the wisdom to make good choices, the courage to stand up for what's right, and a heart that genuinely cares for the people around me. Amen."

CHAPTER 19

Character in Action

You've made it to the end of this book—but really, this is just the beginning.

From the first page, the goal has never been perfection. It's been progress. You've taken a deep dive into the building blocks of strong character—faith, trust, obedience, humility, courage, patience, generosity, and so many others. Each chapter was designed not just to inform, but to transform—to guide you into becoming the person God created you to be.

These character traits were never meant to be learned in isolation. Like a foundation that supports a home, they rely on each other to be effective. As you developed faith, it strengthened your trust. Trust made obedience possible. Obedience shaped conviction. Conviction gave way to courage. And on and on it went. These weren't random lessons—they were intentional steps in building a life that's rooted in something deeper than circumstances or feelings. A life built on *faith*.

But reading isn't enough. Growth comes from putting what you've learned into action.

That's why this book challenged you to reflect, to answer questions honestly, and to take real steps through action challenges. Maybe those parts were difficult. Maybe they forced you to pause, think, pray, and change. That's good. Real growth often begins in discomfort. Each challenge was a chance to stretch your character and let it take shape in your everyday life. The kind of shape that others can see and be impacted by.

Ultimately, strong character isn't just about you—it's about how your life affects the people around you. When you choose to live with integrity, humility, and love, you become a blessing. You become a light. You become someone others trust, admire, and follow—not because you demanded it, but because you earned it.

There's a Cherokee proverb that says, *"When you were born, you cried and the world rejoiced. Live your life so that when you die, the world cries and you rejoice."* That's what character in action looks like. It's living in such a way that your presence makes a lasting difference. It's building your life on a foundation of faith so strong that, even when you're no longer here, the impact of your choices lives on.

So keep growing. Keep learning. Keep applying what you've built. Most importantly, keep reading your Bible. Life isn't about getting it right every time—it's about learning, so that every time you try, you're shaping the kind of life that honors God, strengthens relationships, and brings lasting joy.

"Dear God,

*Thank You for walking with me through this jour-
ney of growth. Thank You for the gift of faith and for
every opportunity to build the character that reflects
Your love and truth. Help me to remember that who I
am becoming matters far more than what I achieve.
Give me strength to live with integrity, courage, patience, and grace. Teach me to lead by serving, to
trust even when I cannot see, and to love even when
it's hard.*

*Shape my heart so that my life makes a lasting dif-
ference—not for my glory, but for Yours. Help me to
live each day with gratitude, humility, and boldness,
honoring the gifts You've given me.*

*May my actions point others toward You, and may
my life be a light that continues shining long after I'm
gone.*

*Thank You for never giving up on me. Keep building
me into the person You created me to be.*

In Jesus' Name, Amen."

This isn't the end. It's your launch point. You are *built on
faith.* Now go live like it.

About the Author

Tyson Gentry is a former Ohio State University football player whose life took an unexpected turn during the spring of his sophomore year. A routine team scrimmage resulted in a spinal cord injury that left him paralyzed from the neck down. Despite the life-altering impact of his injury, Tyson's faith, character, and determination only grew stronger.

After graduating from Ohio State with a degree in Speech and Hearing Science, Tyson went on to earn his master's in Rehabilitation Counseling. In 2014, he founded *New Perspective Foundation*, a nonprofit organization that supports families affected by spinal cord injuries by covering travel expenses so they can remain by their loved one's side during hospitalization and recovery. Since its inception, New Perspective has provided over $700,000 in financial assistance to more than 300 families.

Through his writing and speaking, Tyson empowers young people to live lives of purpose, character, and faith. His unique perspective—shaped by both personal adversity and a deep trust in God—allows him to connect powerfully with audiences of all ages. Built on Faith reflects Tyson's desire to help the next generation build lives that are strong, resilient, and anchored in biblical truth.

Today, as a motivational speaker, Tyson inspires audiences across the nation, sharing his remarkable story of resilience, hope, and mental fortitude. His message encourages others to embrace life's adversities as opportunities for growth, self-discovery, and making a meaningful difference in the world. With unbreakable faith, determination, and a heart full of gratitude, Tyson continues to impact lives, teaching others never to take anything for granted and to seize each day as a new chance to inspire change.

For more information or to invite Tyson to speak at your school, church, or event, please visit www.tysongentry.com.

www.ingramcontent.com/pod-product-compliance
Lightning Source LLC
La Vergne TN
LVHW051124080426
835510LV00018B/2220